SELECTED MEMORIES AND POEMS

—

FORD MADOX FORD

British Library Cataloguing-in-Publication Data
A catalogue record for this book is available from the
British Library

CONTENTS

—

Ford Madox Ford Biography, 1

SELECTED MEMORIES, 3

THE EARLY YEARS, 5

SOME WRITERS AND ARTISTS, 43

POEMS, 139

Ford Madox Ford

Ford Madox Ford was born Ford Hermann Hueffer in London, England in 1873. He grew up in a creative family; his mother was a painter, and his father was an author and a music critic for *The Times* newspaper. Ford's first works were fairy stories. His short tale 'The Brown Owl' was published when he was just eighteen.

Ford met Joseph Conrad when he was twenty-five years old, and the two men became very good friends, co-writing several novels, including *The Inheritors* (1901) and *Romance* (1903). However, The two mens' relationship gradually broke down. A prolific worker, Ford went on to pen a number of works on his own. His *The Good Soldier* (1915) is generally thought of as his best work, and one of the greatest novels of the twentieth century. His *Parade's End* tetralogy (1924–28) and his *The Fifth Queen* trilogy (1906–08) also remain well-regarded.

His writing aside, Ford founded two influential literary journals: *The English Review*, in 1908, and *The Transatlantic*

Review, in 1924. For the latter, Ernest Hemingway became his deputy editor. Together, they published works by prominent writers including Ezra Pound, James Joyce, Gertrude Stein, and Jean Rhys. Throughout this period, Ford continued to write himself. By the end of his career, he had published over eighty books, including fiction, non-fiction and some poetry. Ford died in 1939, aged 65.

SELECTED MEMORIES

Drawn from *Return to Yesterday*,
Ancient Lights, *Mightier than the Sword*,
and *The Heart of the Country*

3

MY GRANDFATHER'S HOUSE

SAYS THACKERAY:

'On his way to the City, Mr Newcome rode to look at the new house, No. 120, Fitzroy Square, which his brother, the colonel, had taken in conjunction with that Indian friend of his, Mr Binnie. . . . The house is vast but, it must be owned, melancholy. Not long since it was a ladies' school, in an unprosperous condition. The scar left by Madame Latour's brass plate may still be seen on the tall black door, cheerfully ornamented, in the style of the end of the last century, with a funereal urn in the centre of the entry, and garlands and the skulls of rams at each corner. . . . The kitchens were gloomy. The stables were gloomy. Great black passages; cracked conservatory; dilapidated bath-room, with melancholy waters moaning and fizzing from the cistern; the great large blank stone staircase—were all so many melancholy features in the general countenance of the house; but the Colonel thought it perfectly cheerful and pleasant, and furnished it in his rough-and-ready way.' *The Newcomes.*

And it was in this house of Colonel Newcome's that my eyes first opened, if not to the light of day, at least to any visual impression that has not since been effaced. I can remember vividly, as a very small boy, shuddering as I stood upon the door-step at the thought that the great stone urn, lichened, soot-stained, and decorated with a great ram's head by way of handle, elevated only by what looked like a square piece of stone of about the size and shape of a folio book, might fall upon me and crush me

5

entirely out of existence. Such a possible happening, I remember, was a frequent subject of discussion among Madox Brown's friends.

Ford Madox Brown, the painter of the pictures called *Work* and *The Last of England,* and the first painter in England, if not in the world, to attempt to render light exactly as it appeared to him, was at that time at the height of his powers, of his reputation, and of such prosperity as he enjoyed. His income from his pictures was considerable, and since he was an excellent talker, an admirable host, extraordinarily and indeed unconscionably open-handed, the great, formal, and rather gloomy house had become a meeting-place for almost all the intellectually unconventional of that time. Between 1870 and 1880 the real Pre-Raphaelite Movement was long since at an end: the Aesthetic Movement, which also was nicknamed Pre-Raphaelite, was, however, coming into prominence, and at the very heart of this movement was Madox Brown. As I remember him, with a square white beard, with a ruddy complexion, and with thick white hair parted in the middle and falling to above the tops of his ears, Madox Brown exactly resembled the king of hearts in a pack of cards. In passion and in emotions—more particularly during one of his fits of gout—he was a hard-swearing, old-fashioned Tory: his reasoning, however, and circumstances made him a revolutionary of the romantic type. I am not sure, even, that toward his later years he would not have called himself an anarchist, and have damned your eyes if you had faintly doubted this obviously extravagant assertion. But he loved the picturesque, as nearly all his friends loved it.

About the inner circle of those who fathered and sponsored the Aesthetic Movement there was absolutely nothing of the languishing. They were, to a man, rather burly, passionate creatures, extraordinarily enthusiastic, extraordinarily romantic, and most impressively quarrelsome. Neither about Rossetti nor about Burne-Jones, neither about William Morris nor P. P. Marshall—and

these were the principal upholders of the firm of Morris
& Company which gave aestheticism to the Western world
—was there any inclination to live upon the smell of the
lily. It was the outer ring, the disciples, who developed
this laudable ambition for poetic pallor, for clinging gar-
ments, and for ascetic countenances. And it was, I believe,
Mr Oscar Wilde who first formulated this poetically vege-
tarian theory of life in Madox Brown's studio at Fitzroy
Square. No, there was little of the smell of the lily about
the leaders of this movement! Thus it was one of Madox
Brown's most pleasing anecdotes—at any rate it was one
that he related with the utmost gusto—how William
Morris came out on to the landing in the house of the
'Firm' in Red Lion Square and roared downstairs:

'Mary, those six eggs were bad. I've eaten them, but
don't let it occur again.'

Morris, also, was in the bait of lunching daily off roast
beef and plum pudding, no matter at what season of the
year, and he liked his puddings large. So that, similarly,
upon the landing one day he shouted:

'Mary, do you call that a pudding?'

He was holding upon the end of a fork a plum pudding
about the size of an ordinary breakfast cup, and having
added some appropriate objurgations, he hurled the edible
downstairs on to Red-Lion Mary's forehead. This anecdote
should not be taken to evidence settled brutality on the
part of the poet-craftsman. Red-Lion Mary was one of the
loyalest supporters of the 'Firm' to the end of her days.
No, it was just in the full-blooded note of the circle. They
liked to swear, and, what is more, they liked to hear each
other swear. Thus, another of Madox Brown's anecdotes
went to show how he kept Morris sitting monumentally
still, under the pretence that he was drawing his portrait,
while Mr Arthur Hughes tied his long hair into knots for
the purpose of enjoying the explosion that was sure to
come when the released Topsy—Morris was always Topsy
to his friends—ran his hands through his hair. This anec-
dote always seemed to me to make considerable calls upon

8+F.M.F. I

one's faith. Nevertheless, it was one that Madox Brown used most frequently to relate, so that no doubt something of the sort must have occurred.

No, the note of these aesthetes was in no sense ascetic. What they wanted in life was room to expand and to be at ease. Thus I remember, in a sort of golden vision, Rossetti lying upon a sofa in the back studio with lighted candles at his feet and lighted candles at his head, while two extremely beautiful ladies dropped grapes into his mouth. But Rossetti did this, not because he desired to present the beholder with a beautiful vision, but because he liked lying on sofas, he liked grapes, and he particularly liked beautiful ladies. They desired, in fact, all of them, room to expand. And when they could not expand in any other directions they expanded enormously into their letters. And—I don't know why—they mostly addressed their letters abusing each other to Madox Brown. There would come one short, sharp note, and then answers occupying reams of note-paper. Thus one great painter would write:

'Dear Brown, Tell Gabriel that if he takes my model Fanny up the river on Sunday I will never speak to him again.'

Gabriel would take the model Fanny up the river on Sunday, and a triangular duel of portentous letters would ensue.

Or again, Swinburne would write:

'Dear Brown, if P. says that I said that Gabriel was in the habit of . . . , P. lies.'

The accusation against Rossetti being a Gargantuan impossibility which Swinburne, surely the most loyal of friends, could impossibly have made, there ensued a Gargantuan correspondence. Brown writes to P. how, when, and why the accusation was made; he explains how he went round to Jones, who had nothing to do with the matter, and found that Jones had eaten practically nothing for the last fortnight, and how between them they had decided that the best thing that they could do would be

8

to go and tell Rossetti all about it, and of how Rossetti
had had a painful interview with Swinburne, and how
unhappy everybody was. P. replies to Brown that he had
never uttered any such words upon any such occasion:
that upon that occasion he was not present, having gone
round to Ruskin, who had the toothache, and who read
him the first hundred and twenty pages of *Stones of
Venice*; that he could not possibly have said anything of
the sort about Gabriel, since he knew nothing whatever
of Gabriel's daily habits, having refused to speak to him
for the last nine months because of Gabriel's intolerable
habit of backbiting, which he was sure would lead them
all to destruction, and so deemed it prudent not to go
near him. Gabriel himself then enters the fray, saying
that he has discovered that it is not P. at all who made
the accusation, but Q., and that the accusation was made
not against him, but about O.X., the Academician. If,
however, he, P., accuses him, Gabriel, of backbiting, P.
must be perfectly aware that this is not the case, he,
Gabriel, having only said a few words against P.'s wife's
mother, who is a damned old cat. And so the correspon-
dence continues, Jones and Swinburne and Marshall and
William Rossetti and Charles Augustus Howell and a
great many more joining in the fray, until at last every-
body withdraws all charges, six months having passed,
and Brown invites all the contestants to dinner, Gabriel
intending to bring old Plint, the picture-buyer, and to
make him, when he has had plenty of wine, buy P.'s
picture of the *Lost Shepherd* for two thousand pounds.

These tremendous quarrels, in fact, were all storms in
teacups, and although the break-up of the 'Firm' did
cause a comparatively lasting estrangement between several
of the partners, it has always pleased me to remember
that at the last private view that Madox Brown held of
one of his pictures, every one of the surviving Pre-
Raphaelite brothers came to his studio, and every one of
the surviving partners of the original firm of Morris &
Company.

The arrival of Sir Edward Burne-Jones and his wife brought up a characteristic passion of Madox Brown's. Sir Edward had persuaded the president of the Royal Academy to accompany them in their visit. They were actuated by the kindly desire to give Madox Brown the idea that thus at the end of his life the Royal Academy wished to extend some sort of official recognition to a painter who had persistently refused for nearly half a century to recognize their existence. Unfortunately it was an autumn day and the twilight had set in very early. Thus not only were the distinguished visitors rather shadowy in the dusk, but the enormous picture itself was entirely indistinguishable. Lady Burne-Jones, with her peculiarly persuasive charm, whispered to me, unheard by Madox Brown, that I should light the studio gas, and I was striking a match, when I was appalled to hear Madox Brown shout, in tones of extreme violence and of apparent alarm:

'Damn and blast it all, Fordie! Do you want us all blown into the next world?'

And he proceeded to explain to Lady Burne-Jones that there was an escape of gas from a pipe. When she suggested candles or a paraffin lamp, Madox Brown declared with equal violence that he couldn't think how she could imagine that he could have such infernally dangerous things in the house. The interview thus concluded in a gloom of the most tenebrous, and shortly afterward we went downstairs, where, in the golden glow of a great many candles set against a golden and embossed wallpaper, tea was being served. The fact was that Madox Brown was determined that no 'damned academician' should see his picture. Nevertheless, it is satisfactory to me to think that there was among these distinguished and kindly men still so great a feeling of solidarity. They had come, many of them from great distances, to do honour, or at least to be kind, to an old painter who at that time was more entirely forgotten than he has ever been before or since.

The 'lily' tradition of the disciples of these men is, I should imagine, almost entirely extinguished. But the other day, at a particularly smart wedding, there turned up one staunch survivor in garments of prismatic hues— a mustard-coloured ulster, a green wide-awake, a blue shirt, a purple tie, and a suit of tweed. This gentleman moved distractedly among groups of correctly attired people. In one hand he bore an extremely minute painting by himself. It was, perhaps, of the size of a visiting-card set in an ocean of white mount. In the other he bore an enormous spray of Madonna lilies. That, I presume, was why he had failed to remove his green hat. He was approached by the hostess, and he told her that he wished to place the picture, his wedding gift, in the most appropriate position that could be found for it. And upon her suggesting that she would attend to the hanging after the ceremony was over, he brushed her aside. Finally he placed the picture upon the ground beneath a tall window, and perched the spray of lilies on top of the frame. He then stood back and, waving his emaciated hands and stroking his brown beard, surveyed the effect of his decoration. The painting, he said, symbolized the consolation that the arts would afford the young couple during their married life, and the lily stood for the purity of the bride. This is how in the 'seventies and the 'eighties the outer ring of the aesthetes really behaved. It was as much in their note as were the plum pudding and the roast beef in William Morris's. The reason for this is not very far to seek. The older men, the Pre-Raphaelites and the members of the 'Firm,' had too rough work to do to bother much about the trimmings.

It is a little difficult nowadays to imagine the acridity with which any new artistic movement was opposed when Victoria was Queen of England. Charles Dickens, as I have elsewhere pointed out, called loudly for the immediate imprisonment of Millais and the other Pre-Raphaelites, including my grandfather, who was not a Pre-Raphaelite. Blasphemy was the charge alleged against them, just as it was the charge alleged against the earliest upholders of Wagner's music in England. This may seem incredible, but I have in my possession three letters from three different members of the public addressed to my father, Dr Francis Hueffer, a man of great erudition and force of character, who, from the early 'seventies until his death, was the musical critic of *The Times*. The writers stated that unless Doctor Hueffer abstained from upholding the blasphemous music of the future—and in each case the writer used the word blasphemous—he would be respectively stabbed, ducked in a horse-pond, and beaten to death by hired roughs. Yet to-day I never go to a place of popular entertainment where miscellaneous music is performed for the benefit of the poorest classes without hearing at least the overture to *Tannhäuser*. Nowadays it is difficult to discern any new movement in any of the arts. No doubt there is movement, no doubt we who write and our friends who paint and compose are producing the arts of the future. But we never have the luck to have the word 'blasphemous' hurled at us. It would, indeed, be almost inconceivable that such a thing could happen, that the frame of mind should be reconstructed. But to the Pre-Raphaelites this word was blessed in the extreme. For human nature is such—perhaps on account of obstinacy or perhaps on account of feelings of justice—that to persecute an art, as to persecute a religion, is simply to render its practitioners the more stubborn and its advocates in their fewness the more united and the more effective in their union. It was the injustice of the attack upon the Pre-Raphaelites, it was the fury and outcry, that won for them the attention of Mr Ruskin. And Mr Ruskin's attention being aroused, he entered on that splendid and efficient championing of their cause which at last established them in a position of perhaps more immediate importance than, as painters, they exactly merited. As pioneers and as sufferers they can never sufficiently be recommended. Mr Ruskin, for some cause which my grandfather was used to declare was purely personal, was the only man intimately connected with these movements who had no connection at all with Madox Brown. I do not know why this was, but it is a fact that, although Madox Brown's pictures were in considerable evidence at all places where the pictures of the Pre-Raphaelites were exhibited, Mr Ruskin in all his works never once mentioned his name. He never blamed him; he never praised him; he ignored him. And this was at a time when Ruskin must have known that a word from him was sufficient to make the fortune of any painter. It was sufficient, not so much because of Mr Ruskin's weight with the general public, as because the small circle of buyers, wealthy and assiduous, who surrounded the painters of the Movement, hung upon Mr. Ruskin's lips and needed at least his printed sanction for all their purchases.

Madox Brown was the most benevolent of men, the most helpful and the kindest. His manifestations, however, were apt at times to be a little thorny. I remember an anecdote which Madox Brown's housemaid of that day was in the habit of relating to me when she used to put me to bed. Said she—and the exact words remain upon my mind:

'I was down in the kitchen waiting to carry up the meat, when a cabman comes down the area steps and says: "I've got your master in my cab. He's very drunk." I says to him'—and an immense intonation of pride would come into Charlotte's voice—' "My master's a-sitting at the head of his table entertaining his guests. That's Mr [Swinburne]. Carry him upstairs and lay him in the bath." '

Madox Brown, whose laudable desire it was at many stages of his career to redeem poets and others from dipsomania, was in the habit of providing several of them with labels upon which were inscribed his own name and address. Thus, when any of these geniuses were found incapable in the neighbourhood they would be brought by cabmen or others to Fitzroy Square. This, I think, was a stratagem more characteristic of Madox Brown's singular

and quaint ingenuity than any that I can recall. The poet
being thus recaptured would be carried upstairs by Char-
lotte and the cabman and laid in the bath—in Colonel
Newcome's very bath-room, where, according to Thacke-
ray, the water moaned and gurgled so mournfully in the
cistern. For me, I can only remember that room as an
apartment of warmth and lightness: it was a concomitant
to all the pleasures that sleeping at my grandfather's meant
for me. And indeed, to Madox Brown as to Colonel New-
come—they were very similar natures in their chivalrous,
unbusinesslike, and naïve simplicity—the house in Fitzroy
Square seemed perfectly pleasant and cheerful.

The poet having been put into the bath would be re-
duced to sobriety by cups of the strongest coffee that could
be made (the bath was selected because he would not be
able to roll out and to injure himself). And having been
thus reduced to sobriety, he would be lectured, and he
would be kept in the house, being given nothing stronger
than lemonade to drink, until he found the régime in-
tolerable. Then he would disappear, the label sewn inside
his coat collar, to reappear once more in the charge of a
cabman.

Of Madox Brown's acerbity I witnessed myself no in-
stances at all, unless it be the one that I have lately
narrated. A possibly too stern father of the old school,
he was as a grandfather extravagantly indulgent. I re-
member his once going through the catalogue of his
grandchildren and deciding, after careful deliberation, that
they were all geniuses with the exception of one, as to
whom he could not be certain whether that one was a
genius or mad. Thus I read with astonishment the words
of a critic of distinction with regard to the exhibition of
Madox Brown's works that I organized at the Grafton
Gallery ten years ago. They were to the effect that Madox
Brown's pictures were very crabbed and ugly—but what
was to be expected of a man whose disposition was so
harsh and distorted? This seemed to me to be an amazing
statement. But upon discovering the critic's name I found

that Madox Brown once kicked him downstairs. The
gentleman in question had come to Madox Brown with
the proposal from an eminent firm of picture-dealers that
the painter should sell all his works to them for a given
number of years at a very low price. In return they were
to do what would be called nowadays 'booming' him, and
they would do their best to get him elected as Associate
of the Royal Academy. That Madox Brown should have
received with such violence a proposition that seemed to
the critic so eminently advantageous for all parties, justi-
fied that gentleman in his own mind in declaring that
Madox Brown had a distorted temperament. Perhaps he
had.

But if he had a rough husk he had a sweet kernel, and
for this reason the gloomy house in Fitzroy Square did
not, I think, remain as a shape of gloom in the minds of
many people. It was very tall, very large, very grey, and
in front of it towered up very high the mournful plane-
trees of the square. And over the porch was the funereal
urn with the ram's heads. This object, dangerous and
threatening, has always seemed to me to be symbolical
of this circle of men, so practical in their work and so
romantically unpractical, as a whole, in their lives. They
knew exactly how, according to their lights, to paint
pictures, to write poems, to make tables, to decorate
pianos, rooms, or churches. But as to the conduct of life
they were a little sketchy, a little romantic, perhaps a little
careless. I should say that of them all Madox Brown was
the most practical. But his way of being practical was
always to be quaintly ingenious. Thus we had the urn.
Most of the Pre-Raphaelites dreaded it: they all of them
talked about it as a possible danger, but never was any
step taken for its removal. It was never even really settled
in their minds whose would be the responsibility for any
accident. It is difficult to imagine the frame of mind, but
there it was and there to this day the urn remains. The
question could have been settled by any lawyer, or Madox
Brown might have had some clause that provided for his

8*

indemnity inserted in his lease. And, just as the urn itself set the tone of the old immense Georgian mansion fallen from glory, so perhaps the fact that it remained for so long the topic of conversation set the note of the painters, the painter-poets, the poet-craftsmen, the painter-musicians, the filibuster verse-writers, and all that singular collection of men versed in the arts. They assembled and revelled comparatively modestly in the rooms where Colonel Newcome and his fellow directors of the Bundelcund Board had partaken of mulligatawny and spiced punch before the sideboard that displayed its knife-boxes with the green-handled knives in their serried phalanxes.

But, for the matter of that, Madox Brown's own sideboard also displayed its green-handled knives, which always seemed to me to place him as the man of the old school in which he was born and remained to the end of his days. If he was impracticable, he hadn't about him a touch of the Bohemian; if he was romantic, his romances took place along ordered lines. Every friend's son of his who went into the navy was destined in his eyes to become, not a pirate, but at least a port-admiral. Every young lawyer that he knew was certain, even if he were only a solicitor, to become Lord Chancellor, and every young poet who presented him with a copy of his first work was destined for the laureateship. And he really believed in these romantic prognostications, which came from him without end as without selection. So that if he was the first to give a helping hand to D. G. Rossetti, his patronage in one or two other instances was not so wisely bestowed.

He was, of course, the sworn foe of the Royal Academy. For him they were always, the members of that august body, 'those *damned* academicians,' with a particular note of acerbity upon the expletive. Yet I very well remember, upon the appearance of the first numbers of the *Daily Graphic*, that Madox Brown, being exceedingly struck by the line engravings of one of the artists whom that paper regularly employed to render social functions, exclaimed: 'By Jove! if young Cleaver goes on as well as he has

16

begun, those damned academicians, supposing they had any sense, would elect him president right away!' Thus it will be seen that the business of romance was not to sweep away the Royal Academy, was not to found an opposing salon. It was to capture the established body by storm, leaping as it were on to the very quarter-deck, and setting to the old ship a new course. The characteristic, in fact, of all these men was their warm-heartedness, their enmity for the formal, for the frigid, for the ungenerous. It cannot be said that any of them despised money. I doubt whether it would even be said that any of them did not, at one time or another, seek for popularity, or try to paint, write, or decorate pot-boilers. But they were naïvely unable to do it. To the timid—and the public is always the timid—what was individual in their characters was always alarming. It was alarming even when they tried to paint the conventional dog-and-girl pictures of the Christmas supplement. The dogs were too like dogs and did not simper; the little girls were too like little girls. They would be probably rendered as just losing their first teeth.

In spite of the Italianism of Rossetti, who was never in Italy, and the mediaevalism of Morris, who had never looked mediaevalism, with its cruelties, its filth, its stenches, and its avarice, in the face—in spite of these tendencies that were forced upon them by those two contagious spirits, the whole note of this old, romantic circle was national, was astonishingly English, was Georgian even. They seemed to date from the Regency, and to have skipped altogether the baneful influences of early Victorianism and of the commerciality that the Prince Consort spread through England. They seem to me to resemble in their lives—and perhaps in their lives they were greater than their works—to resemble nothing so much as a group of old-fashioned ships' captains. Madox Brown, indeed, was nominated for a midshipman in the year 1827. His father had fought on the famous *Arethusa* in the classic fight with the *Belle Poule*. And but for the fact that his father quarrelled with Commodore Coffin, and so lost all hope of influence at the Admiralty, it is probable that Madox Brown would never have painted a picture or have lived in Colonel Newcome's house. Indeed, on the last occasion when I saw William Morris I happened to meet him in Portland Place. He was going to the house of a peer that his firm was engaged in decorating, and he took me with him to look at the work. He was then a comparatively old man, and his work had grown very flamboyant, so that the decoration of the dining-room consisted, as far as I can remember, of one huge acanthus-leaf design. Morris looked at this absent-mindedly, and said that he had just been talking to some members of a ship's crew whom he had met in Fenchurch Street. They had remained for some time under the impression that he was a ship's captain. This had pleased him very much, for it was his ambition to be taken for such a man. I have heard, indeed, that this happened to him on several occasions, on each of which he expressed an equal satisfaction. With a grey beard like the foam of the sea, with grey hair through which he continually ran his hands erect and curly on his forehead, with a hooked nose, a florid complexion, and clean, clear eyes, dressed in a blue serge coat, and carrying, as a rule, a satchel, to meet him was always, as it were, to meet a sailor ashore. And that in essence was the note of them all. When they were at work they desired that everything they did should be shipshape; when they set their work down they became like Jack ashore. And perhaps that is why there is, as a rule, such a scarcity of artists in England. Perhaps to what is artistic in the nation the sea has always called too strongly.

MY NURSE, MRS ATTERBURY

My nurse, Mrs Atterbury, had one singularity—she had come in contact with more murders and deaths by violence than any person I ever met—at any rate until 1914. In consequence, I imagine, my childhood was haunted by imaginary horrors and was most miserable. I can still see the shadows of wolves if I lie awake in bed with a fire in the room. And indeed I had the fixed belief for years that except for myself the world was peopled with devils. I used to peep through the cracks of doors to see the people within in their natural forms.

Mrs Atterbury had been in the great railway accident near Doncaster where innumerable persons were burned to death; she had seen seven people run over and killed and her milder conversations abounded in details of deaths by drowning. I don't think she was present at the sinking of the *Princess Alice* but she talked about it as if she had been. Her normal conversations ran:

'When I lived with meyuncle Power in the Minories time of the Crimea Wower, meyuncle let 'is top front to a master saddler. N'wen wower broke out the master saddler 'e worked niteanday, niteanday fer sevin weeks without stop er stay. N'e took 'is saddles to the Wower Orfis 'n drawed his pay. All in gowlden sovrins in a Gledstun beg. N'wen 'e got 'ome 'e cut 'is froat on the top front landin' 'n the blood 'n the gowld run down the staircase together like the awtificial cascades in Battersea Pawk.'. . . 'The blood 'n the gowld!'. . . she would repeat and catch my wrist in her skinny fingers.

She was a witness—or an almost witness—of one of the Jack the Ripper murders in Whitechapel. She certainly came on the body of one of the victims and claimed to have seen a man vanish into the fog. I never actually heard the details of that. My mother, worried by the advent of a questioning police sergeant and the hysterics of the household below stairs, forbade the old lady to tell us children about it. But her impressive and mysterious absence in her best black bonnet and jet beaded cloak, and the whispers of the household, made me fully aware that she was giving evidence at the Inkwedge. For long afterwards heaven knew what horrors were not concealed for me in the pools of shadow beneath the lamp-posts. In solitary streets your footsteps echoing and a smudge of fog in the gaslight!

The last time I saw the old lady she was sitting—as she did day in day out for years—in the window of a parlour that occupied the apex of a corner lot in an outer suburb. She could look right up and down two long streets.

She greeted me with great vivacity. The day before there had been a tremendous thunderstorm. The streets up which she looked had been almost obscured by falling water. She said to me:

'I calls out to Lizzie. . . . Good gracious me! That man! " 'E's struck dead!" . . . N'e *was*!' she added triumphantly.

MY COUSINS, THE ROSSETTIS

My cousins, the Rossettis, were horrible monsters of precocity. Let me set down here with what malignity I viewed their proficiency in Latin and Greek at ages incredibly small. Thus, I believe, my cousin Olive wrote a Greek play at the age of something like five. And, they were perpetually being held up to us—or perhaps to myself alone, for my brother was always very much the sharper of the two—as marvels of genius whom I ought to thank God for merely having the opportunity to emulate. For my cousin Olive's infernal Greek play which had to do with Theseus and the Minotaur, draped in robes of the most flimsy butter muslin, I was drilled, a lanky boy of twelve or so, to wander round and round the back drawing-room of Endsleigh Gardens, imbecilely flapping my naked arms before an audience singularly distinguished who were seated in the front room. The scenery which had been designed and painted by my aunt was, I believe, extremely beautiful; and the chinoiseries, the fine furniture and the fine pictures were such that had I been allowed to sit peaceably amongst the audience, I might really have enjoyed the piece. But it was my unhappy fate to wander round in the garb of a captive before an audience that consisted of Pre-Raphaelite poets, ambassadors of foreign powers, editors, poets laureate, and Heaven knows what. Such formidable beings at least did they appear to my childish imagination. From time to time the rather high voice of my father would exclaim from the gloomy depths of the auditorium, 'Speak up, Fordie!' Alas, my aptitude for that sort of sport being limited, the only words that were allotted to me were the Greek lamentation, 'Theu! Theu! Theu!' and in the meanwhile my cousin Arthur Rossetti, who appeared only to come up to my knee, was the hero Theseus, strode about with a large sword, slew dragons and addressed perorations in the Tennysonian 'o' and 'a' style, to the candle-lit heavens, with their distant view of Athens. Thank God, having been an adventurous youth whose sole idea of true joy was to emulate the doings of the hero of a work called *Peck's Bad Boy and His Pa*, or at least to attain to the lesser glories of Dick Harkaway, who had a repeating rifle and a tame black jaguar and who bathed in gore almost nightly—thank God, I say, that we succeeded in leading our unsuspecting cousins into dangerous situations from which they only emerged by breaking limbs. I seem to remember the young Rossettis as perpetually going about with fractured bones. I distinctly remember the fact that I bagged my cousin Arthur with one collar-bone, broken on a boat slide in my company, whilst my younger sister brought down her cousin Mary with a broken elbow fractured in a stone hall. Olive Rossetti, I also remember with gratification, cut her head open at a party given by Miss Mary Robinson because she wanted to follow me down some dangerous steps and fell on to a flower-pot.

POETESSES IN FOUR-WHEELERS

The poet—and still more the poetess—of the 'seventies and 'eighties, though an awful, was a frail creature who had to be carried about from place to place, and generally in a four-wheeled cab. Indeed, if my recollection of these poetesses in my very earliest days was accompanied always by thunders and congratulations, my images of them in slightly later years, when I was not so strictly confined to the nursery—my images of them were always those of somewhat elderly ladies, forbidding in aspect, with grey hair, hooked noses, flashing eyes, and continued trances of indignation against reviewers. They emerged ungracefully —for no one ever yet managed to emerge gracefully from the door of a four-wheeler—sometimes backwards from one of those creaking and dismal tabernacles and pulling behind them odd-shaped parcels. Holding the door open, with his whip in one hand, would stand the cabman. He wore an infinite number of little capes on his overcoat; a grey worsted muffler would be coiled many times round his throat and the lower part of his face, and his top hat would be of some unglossy material that I have never been able to identify. After a short interval his hand would become extended, the flat palm displaying such coins as the poetess had laid in it. And, when the poetess with her odd bundles was three-quarters of the way up the door-steps, the cabman, a man of the slowest and most deliberate, would be pulling the muffler down from about his mouth and exclaiming:

'Wot's this?'

The poetess without answering, but with looks of enormous disdain, would scuffle into the house and the front door would close. Then upon the knocker the cabman would commence his thunderous symphony.

Somewhat later more four-wheelers would arrive with more poetesses. Then still more four-wheelers with elderly poets; untidy-looking young gentlemen with long hair and wide-awake hats, in attitudes of dejection and fatigue would ascend the steps; a hansom or two would drive up containing rather smarter, stout elderly gentlemen wearing, as a rule, black coats with velvet collars and most usually black gloves. These were reviewers, editors of the *Athenaeum* and of other journals. Then there would come quite smart gentlemen with an air of prosperity in their clothes, and with deference somewhat resembling that of undertakers in their manners. These would be publishers.

You are to understand that what was about to proceed was the reading to this select gathering of the latest volume of poems by Mrs Clara Fletcher—that is not the name— the authoress of what was said to be a finer sequence of sonnets than those of Shakespeare. And before a large semicircle of chairs occupied by the audience that I have described, and, with Mr Clara Fletcher standing obsequiously behind her to hand her, from the odd-shaped bundles of manuscripts, the pages that she required, Mrs Clara Fletcher, with her regal head regally poised, having quelled the assembly with a single glance, would commence to read.

Mournfully then, up and down the stone staircases there would flow two hollow sounds. For in those days it was the habit of all poets and poetesses to read aloud upon every possible occasion, and whenever they read aloud to employ an imitation of the voice invented by the late Lord Tennyson, and known in those days as the *ore rotundo*— 'with the round mouth mouthing out their hollow o's and a's.'

The effect of this voice heard from outside a door was to a young child particularly awful. It went on and on, suggesting the muffled baying of a large hound that is permanently dissatisfied with the world. And this awful rhythm would be broken in upon from time to time by the thunders of the cabman. How the housemaid—the house-maid was certainly Charlotte Kirby—dealt with this man of wrath I never could rightly discover. Apparently the cabman would thunder upon the door; Charlotte, keeping it on the chain, would open it for about a foot. The cabman would exclaim, 'Wot's this?' and Charlotte would shut the door in his face. The cabman would remain inactive for four minutes in order to recover his breath. Then once more his stiff arm would approach the knocker and again the thunders would resound. The cabman would exclaim: 'A bob and a tanner from the Elephant and Castle to Tottenham Court Road!' and Charlotte would again close the door in his face. This would continue for perhaps half an hour. Then the cabman would drive away to meditate. Later he would return and the same scenes would be gone through. He would retire once more for more meditation and return in the company of a policeman. Then Charlotte would open the front door wide and by doing no more than ejaculate 'My good man!' she would appear to sweep out of existence policeman, cab, cabhorse, cabman, and whip. A settled peace would descend upon the house, lulled into silence by the reverberation of the hollow o's and a's. In about five minutes' time the policeman would return and converse amiably with Charlotte for three-quarters of an hour, through the area railings. I suppose that was really why cabmen were always worsted and poetesses protected from these importunities in the dwelling over whose destinies Charlotte presided for forty years.

THE ABBÉ LISZT

When I was a very small boy indeed I was taken to a concert. In those days, as a token of my Pre-Raphaelite origin, I wore very long golden hair, a suit of greenish-

yellow corduroy velveteen with gold buttons, and two
stockings of which the one was red and the other green.
These garments were the curse of my young existence and
the joy of every street-boy who saw me. I was taken to this
concert by my father's assistant on *The Times* newspaper.
Mr Rudall was the most kindly, the most charming, the
most gifted, the most unfortunate—and also the most
absent-minded—of men. Thus, when we had arrived in
our stalls—and in those days the representative of *The
Times* always had the two middle front seats—Mr Rudall
discovered that he had omitted to put on his neck-tie that
day. He at once went out to purchase one, and, having
become engrossed in the selection, he forgot all about the
concert, went away to the Thatched House Club, and
passed there the remainder of the evening. I was left, in
the middle of the front row, all alone and feeling very tiny
and deserted, the sole representative of the august organ
that in those days was known as the Thunderer.

Immediately in front of me, standing in the vacant space
before the platform, which was all draped in red, there
were three gilt arm-chairs and a gilt table. In the hall there
was a great and continuing rustle of excitement. Then,
suddenly, this became an enormous sound of applause. It
volleyed and rolled round and round the immense space;
I had never heard such a sound and I have never again
heard such another. Then I perceived that from beneath
the shadow of the passage that led into the artistes' room—
in the deep shadow—there had appeared a silver head, a
dark brown face, hook-nosed, smiling the enigmatic,
Jesuit's smile, the long locks falling backwards so that
the whole shape of the apparition was that of the Sphynx
head. Behind this figure came two others that excited no
proportionate attention, but, small as I then was, I recog-
nized in them the late King and the present Queen
Mother.

They came closer and closer to me; they stood in front
of the three gilt arm-chairs; the deafening applause

continued. The old man with the terrible enigmatic face made gestures of modesty. He refused, smiling all the time, to sit in one of the gilt arm-chairs. And suddenly he bowed down upon me. He stretched out his hands; he lifted me out of my seat, he sat down in it himself and left me standing, the very small lonely child with the long golden curls, underneath all those eyes and stupefied by the immense sounds of applause.

The King sent an equerry to entreat the Master to come to his seat; the Master sat firmly planted there smiling obstinately. Then the Queen came and took him by the hand. She pulled him—I don't know how much strength she needed—right out of his seat and—to prevent his returning to it she sat down there. After all it was *my* seat. And then, as if she realized my littleness and my loneliness, she drew me to her and set me on her knee. It was a gracious act.

There is a passage in Pepys's *Diary* in which he records that he was present at some excavations in Westminster Abbey when they came upon the skull of Jane Seymour, and he kissed the skull on the place where once the lips had been. And in his *Diary* he records: 'It was on such and such a day of such and such a year that I did kiss a Queen,' and then, his feelings overcoming him, he repeats: 'It was on such and such a day of such and such a year that I did kiss a Queen'—I have forgotten what was the date when I sat in a Queen's lap. But I remember very well that when I came out into Piccadilly the cabmen, with their three-tiered coats, were climbing up the lamp-posts and shouting out: 'Three cheers for the Habby Liszt!' And indeed the magnetic personality of the Abbé Liszt was incredible in its powers of awakening enthusiasm.

A few days later my father took me to call at the house where Liszt was staying—it was at the Lytteltons', I suppose. There were a number of people in the drawing-room and they were all asking Liszt to play. Liszt steadfastly refused. A few days before he had had a slight accident that had hurt one of his hands. Suddenly he turned his eyes upon me, and then, bending down, he said in my ear:

'Little boy, I will play for you, so that you will be able to tell your children's children that you have heard Liszt play.'

And he played the first movement of the *Moonlight Sonata*. I do not remember much of his playing, but I remember very well that I was looking, whilst Liszt played, at a stalwart, florid Englishman who is now an earl. And suddenly I perceived that tears were rolling down his cheeks. And soon all the room was in tears. It struck me as odd that people should cry because Liszt was playing the *Moonlight Sonata*.

Ah! that wonderful personality; there was no end to the enthusiasms it aroused. I had a distant connection—oddly enough an English one—who became by marriage a lady-in-waiting at the Court of Saxe-Weimar. I met her a few years ago, and she struck me as a typically English and unemotional personage. But she had always about her a disagreeable odour that persisted to the day of her death. When they came to lay her out, they discovered that round her neck she wore a sachet, and in that sachet there was the half of a cigar that had been smoked by Liszt. Liszt had lunched with her and her husband thirty years before.

A PRE-RAPHAELITE POETESS

One of the other most unpleasant memories of mine were the incursions made upon me by a Pre-Raphaelite poetess, Miss Mathilde Blind. Miss Blind was descended from a distinguished family of revolutionaries. Indeed, one of the brothers attempted to assassinate Bismarck, and disappeared, without any trace of him ever again being heard of, in the dungeons of a Prussian fortress. She was, moreover, a favourite pupil of Mazzini the liberator of Italy, and a person, in her earlier years, of extreme beauty and fire. Upon the death of their son and the marriage of their two daughters, the late Mrs William Rossetti and Mrs Francis Hueffer, the Madox Browns adopted Mathilde Blind who from thenceforward spent most of her time with them. As a boy—I wrote my first book when I was sixteen and its success alas! was more tremendous than any that I can ever again know—I would be sitting in my little study either upon my writing or my school tasks, when ominous sounds would be heard at the door. Miss Blind, with her magnificent aquiline features and fine grey hair, would enter, alarming slip proofs dangling from both her hands. 'Fordie,' she would say, 'I want a synonym for "dun."' On page 152 of her then volume of poems she would have written of dun cows standing in green streams. She was then correcting the proofs of page 154 to find that she had spoken of the dun cows returning homewards over the leas. Some other adjective would have to be found for this useful quadruped. Then my bad quarter of an hour would commence. I would suggest 'strawberry-coloured' and she would say that that would not fit the metre. I would try 'roan' but she would say that that would spoil the phonetic syzygy. I did not know what that was but I would next suggest 'heifers,' whereupon she would say that heifers did not give milk and that, anyhow, the accentuation was wrong. I would be reduced to a miserable muteness; Miss Blind frightened me out of my life. And rising up and gathering her proof-sheets together, the poetess, with her Medusa head, would regard me with indignant and piercing brown eyes. 'Fordie,' she would say with an awful scrutiny, 'your grandfather says you are a genius, but I have never been able to discover in you any signs but those of your being as stupid as a donkey.' I never *could* escape from being likened to that other useful quadruped.

MY UNHAPPIEST NIGHT

I remember as a boy being set somewhat inconsiderately the task of convoying home a very distinguished artist, practising, however, an art other than that of poetry. We had been at a musical evening in the neighbourhood of Swiss Cottage and arrived at the Underground Station just before the last train came in. My enormously distinguished temporary ward was in the habit of filling one of his trouser pockets with chocolate creams and the other with large, unset diamonds. With the chocolate creams he was accustomed to solace his sense of taste whilst he sat in the artistes' room waiting for his turn to play. With the diamonds on similar occasions he solaced his sense of touch, plunging his hand amongst them and moving them about luxuriously. He would have sometimes as many as twenty or thirty large and valuable stones. On this occasion M., always an excitable person, was in a state of extreme rage. For at the party where he had played M. Saint-Saens the composer had also been invited to play the piano. As far as I can remember Saint-Saens was not a very good pianist; he had the extremely hard touch of the organist, and M. considered that to have invited him to sit down on the same piano-stool was an insult almost beyond bearing.

The platform of the Underground Railway was more than usually gloomy, since, the last down train having gone, the lamps upon the other platform had been extinguished. M. volleyed and thundered, and at last, just as the train came in, he thrust both his hands into his trouser pockets and then waved them wildly above his head in execration of my insufficient responsiveness. There flew from the one pocket a shower of chocolate creams, from the other a shower of diamonds. M. gave a final scream upon a very high note and plunged into a railway carriage. I was left divided as to whether my duty were towards the maestro or his jewels. I suppose it was undue materialism in myself, but I stayed to look after the diamonds. It was a long and agonizing search. The station-master, who imagined that I was as mad as the vanished musician, insisted that there were no diamonds and extinguished the station lamps. A friendly porter, however, assisted me with a hand-lantern and eventually we recovered about five diamonds, each perhaps as large as my little finger-nail. Whether any more remained upon the platform I never knew, for M. also never knew how many jewels he possessed or carried about him. It was a night certainly of nightmare, for being so young a boy I had not sufficient money to take a cab and the last train into Town had gone. I had, therefore, to walk to Claridge's Hotel, a distance of perhaps four miles, and arriving there I could not discover that the porter had seen anything of M. I therefore thought it wise to arouse his wife. Mme. —— was accustomed to being awakened at all hours of the night. Her distinguished husband was in the habit of dragging her impetuously out of bed to listen to his latest rendering of a passage of Chopin; and indeed upon this account, she subsequently divorced the master, such actions being held by the French courts to constitute incompatibility of temperament. She did not, however, take my arousing her with any the greater equanimity, and when I produced the diamonds she upbraided me violently for having lost the master. There ensued a more agonizing period of driving about in cabs before we discovered M. detained at the police station nearest Baker Street. He had in his vocabulary no English at all except some very startling specimens of profanity. Upon arriving at Baker Street Station he had spent a considerable amount of time and energy in attempting to explain to the ticket collector in French that he had lost a sacred charge, a weakly little boy incapable of taking care of himself; and as he did not even know the name of his hotel the police had taken charge of him and were attempting kindly to keep him soothed by singing popular songs to him in the charge-room where we found him quite contented and happy, beating time with his feet to the melody of 'Two Lovely Black Eyes.' I think this was upon the whole the unhappiest night I ever spent.

THE MUSIC CRITIC OF *THE TIMES*

In England, at any rate in the musical world, as in the world of all the other arts, a general change seems gradually to have come over the atmosphere in the last quarter of a century. Jealousies amongst executants, amongst composers, have diminished; and along with them have diminished the enthusiasm and the partisanships of the public. In the 'fifties and 'sixties there was an extraordinary outcry against the Pre-Raphaelite movement, in the 'seventies and 'eighties there was an outcry almost more extraordinary against what was called the Music of the Future. As I have said elsewhere, Charles Dickens attempted to get the authorities to imprison the Pre-Raphaelite painters because he considered that their works were blasphemous. And he was backed by a whole, great body of public opinion. In the 'seventies and 'eighties there were cries for the imprisonment alike of the critics who upheld and the artistes who performed the Music of the Future. The compositions of Wagner were denounced as being atheistic, sexually immoral, and tending to further socialism and the throwing of bombs. Wagnerites were threatened with assassination, and assaults between critics of the rival schools were things not unknown in the foyer of the opera. I really believe that my father, as the chief exponent of Wagner in these islands, did go in some personal danger. Extraordinary pressures were brought to bear upon the more prominent critics of the day, the pressure coming, as a rule, from the exponents of the school of Italian opera. Thus, at the openings of the opera seasons packing-cases of large dimensions and considerable

31

in number would arrive at the house of the ferocious critic
of the chief newspaper of England. They would contain
singular assortments of comestibles and of objects of art.
Thus I remember half a dozen hams, the special product
of some north Italian town, six cases of Rhine wine, which
were no doubt intended to propitiate the malignant
Teuton; a reproduction of the Medici Venus in marble,
painted with phosphoric paint so that it gleamed blue and
ghostly in the twilight; a case of Bohemian glass and
several strings of Italian sausages. And these packing cases,
containing no outward sign of their senders, would have
to be unpacked and then once more repacked, leaving the
servants with fingers damaged by nails and passages littered
with straw. Inside would be found the cards of Italian
prime donne, tenors or basses, newly arrived in London,
and sending servile homage to the illustrious critic of the
'Giornale Times.' On one occasion a letter containing
bank-notes for £50 arrived from a *prima donna* with a
pathetic note begging the critic to absent himself from her
first night. Praise from a Wagnerite she considered to be
impossible, but she was ready to pay for silence. I do not
know whether this letter inspired my father with the idea
of writing to the next suppliant that he was ready to accept
her present—it was the case of Bohemian glass—but that
in that case he would never write a word about her singing.
He meant the letter, of course, as a somewhat clumsy joke,
but the lady—she was not, however, an Italian—possessing
a sense of humour, at once accepted the offer. This put my
father rather in a quandary, for Mme. H—— was one of
the greatest exponents of emotional tragic music that there
had ever been, and the occasion on which she was to appear
was the first performance in England of one of the great
operas of the world. I do not exactly know whether my
father went through any conscientious troubles—I presume
he did, for he was a man of singular moral niceness. At any
rate he wrote an enthusiastic notice of the opera and an
enthusiastic and deserved notice of the impersonatrix of
Carmen. And since the Bohemian glass—or the poor re-

mains of the breakages of a quarter of a century—still decorate my sideboard, I presume that he accepted the present. I do not really see what else he could have done.

Pressure of other sorts was also not unknown. Thus, there was an opera produced by a foreign baron who was a distinguished figure in the diplomatic service, and who was very well looked on at Court. In the middle of the performance my father received a command to go into the royal box, where a royal personage informed him that in his august opinion the work was one of genius. My father replied that he was sorry to differ from so distinguished a connoisseur—but that in his opinion the music was absolute rubbish—*Lauter Klatsch*. The reply was undiplomatic and upon the whole regrettable, but my father had been irritated by the fact that a good deal of Court pressure had already been brought to bear upon him. I believe that there were diplomatic reasons for desiring to flatter the composer of the opera, who was attached to a foreign embassy—the embassy of the nation with whom for the moment the diplomatic relations of Great Britain were somewhat strained. So that without doubt His Royal Highness was as patriotically in the right as my father was in a musical sense. Eventually, the notice of the opera was written by another hand. The performance of this particular opera remains in my mind because during one of its scenes, which represented the frozen circle of Hell, the cotton wool, which figures as snow on the stage, caught fire and began to burn. An incipient panic took place among the audience, but the orchestra, under a firm composer whose name I have unfortunately forgotten, continued to play, and the flames were extinguished by one of the singers using his cloak. But I still remember being in the back of the box and seeing in the foreground, silhouetted against the lights of the stage, the figures of my father and of some one else—I think it was William Rossetti—standing up and shouting down into the stalls: 'Sit down, brutes! Sit down, cowards!'

On the other hand, it is not to be imagined that acts of kindness and good-fellowship were rare under this seething mass of passions and of jealousies. Thus at one of the Three Choir Festivals, my father, having had the misfortune to sprain his ankle, was unable to be present in the cathedral. His notice was written for him by the critic of the paper which was most violently opposed to views at all Wagnerian—a gentleman whom till that moment my father regarded as his bitterest personal enemy. This critic happened to be staying in the same hotel, and having heard of the accident volunteered to write the notice out of sheer good feeling. This gentleman, an extreme *bon vivant* and a man of an excellent and versatile talent, has since told me that he gave himself particular trouble to imitate my father's slightly cumbrous Germanic English and his extreme modernist views. This service was afterwards repaid by my father in the following circumstances. It was again one of the Three Choir Festivals—at Worcester, I think, and we were stopping at Malvern—my father and Mr S—— going in every day to the cathedral city. Mr S—— was either staying with us or in an adjoining house, and on one Wednesday evening, his appetite being sharpened by an unduly protracted performance of 'The Messiah,' Mr S—— partook so freely of the pleasures of the table that he omitted altogether to write his notice. This fact he remembered just before the closing of the small local telegraph office, and although Mr S—— was by no means in a condition to write his notice, he was yet sufficiently mellow with wine to be lachrymose and overwhelmed at the idea of losing his post. We rushed off at once to the telegraph office and did what we could to induce the officials to keep the wires open whilst the notice was being written. But all inducements failed. My father hit upon a stratagem at the last moment. At that date it was a rule of the Post Office that if the beginning of a long message were handed in before eight o'clock the office must be kept open until its conclusion as long as there was no break in the handing in of slips. My father therefore commanded me to telegraph anything that I liked to the newspaper office as long as I kept it up whilst he was writing the notice of 'The Messiah.' And the only thing that came into my head at the moment was the Church Service. The newspaper was therefore astonished to receive a long telegram beginning! *When the wicked man turneth away from the sin that he has committed* and continuing through the *Te Deum* and the *Nunc Dimittis,* till suddenly it arrived at 'The Three Choirs Festival. Worcester, Wednesday, July 27th, 1887.'

A GERMAN MASTER

At the last public school which I attended—for my attendances at schools were varied and singular, according as my father ruined himself with starting new periodicals or happened to be flush of money on account of new legacies—at my last public school I was permitted to withdraw myself every afternoon to go to concerts. This brought down upon me the jeers of one particular German master who kept order in the afternoons, and upon one occasion he set for translation the sentence:

'Whilst I was idling away my time at a concert, the rest of my classmates were diligently engaged in study of the German language.'

Proceeding mechanically with the translation—for I paid no particular attention to Mr P——, because my father, in his reasonable tones, had always taught me that schoolmasters were men of inferior intelligence to whom personally we should pay little attention, though the rules for which they stood must be exactly observed—I had got as far as *Indem ich faulenzte* ... when it suddenly occurred to me that Mr P—— in setting this sentence to the class was aiming a direct insult not only at myself, but at Beethoven, Bach, Mozart, Wagner, and Robert Franz.

An extraordinary and now inexplicable fury overcame me.
At all my schools I was always the good boy of my respec-
tive classes, but on this occasion I rose in my seat pro-
pelled by an irresistible force, and I addressed Mr P——
with words the most insulting and the most contemptuous.
I pointed out that music was the most divine of all arts,
that German was a language fit only for horses; that
German literature contained nothing that any sensible
person could want to read except the works of Schopen-
hauer, who was an anglomaniac, and in any case was much
better read in an English translation; I pointed out that
Victor Hugo has said that to utter the lowest type of
inanities, '*il faut être stupide comme un maître d'école
qui n'est bon à rien que pour planter des choux.*' I can
still feel the extraordinary indignation that filled me,
though I have to make an effort of the imagination to
understand why I was so excited; I can still feel the way
the breath poured through my distended nostrils. With,
I suppose, some idea of respect for discipline I had care-
fully spoken in German which none of my classmates
understood. My harangue was suddenly ended by Mr
P——'s throwing his large inkpot at me; it struck me
upon the shoulder and ruined my second-best coat and
waistcoat.

THE PINES, PUTNEY

Well, Time went on; my father died; Mr Watts-Dunton
became my mother's trustee and my guardian. He also
threw his comether over Mr Swinburne and took him to
live with him in the Pines, Putney. There they both grew
deaf together under the housekeepership of Mr Watts-
Dunton's sister, the widow of an attorney who had not
made good—in a white, high, widow's cap, white mittens,
and a black silk shoulder-cape. Deaf, too. . . . You may

imagine all three deaf people sitting together in the dusk cf the Pines waiting for the argand colza-oil lamp to be lighted, when Mr Swinburne and Mrs Mason would play cribbage whilst the poet sipped his glass of Worcester Sauce and Mr Watts-Dunton pored over a crabbed volume of forgotten gipsy lore . . . or made pretence so to do.

The Pines, Putney, as its name shows, was no place for the stabling of Pegasus. It was, upon the whole, the most lugubrious London semi-detached villa that it was ever my fate to enter. It was spacious enough, but, built at the time of the 1850–60 craze for Portland cement, its outer surfaces had collected enough soot to give it the aspect of the dwelling of a workhouse master or chief gaoler. In the sooty garden grew a single fir that, in my time at least, could have gone as a Christmas tree into the villa's dining-room. In the next garden there had been another, but that had died.

I don't mean to say that the house was poverty-stricken. It was the residence of the highly prosperous family lawyer that Mr Watts-Dunton was, well staffed with servants, the windows and furniture always kept at a high pitch of polish, the cut steel fire implements always shining . . . I imagine the walls must have been covered with brown paper in the proper aesthetic fashion of the advanced of the day and that that drank up the light. . . . At any rate the rooms of the Pines, Putney, were always dim . . . I had occasion to go there pretty frequently . . . once a quarter at least when my mother's dividends were due; and on occasion when she had outrun the constable and needed an advance . . . or when I myself did! . . . So it was pretty often.

Then I would be received with an extraordinary pomp of praise by Mr Watts-Dunton. He would address to me studied periods of adulation of my latest published book. . . . I had published I think six before I came of age . . . and Mr Watts-Dunton addressed me as if I were a public meeting. And Mr Swinburne would add some nervous phrases to the effect that he intended to read my book

as soon as time served.... He would be floating some-
where about in the dimnesses like a shaft of golden
light.... But when I came seriously to prefer my request
for a cheque and Mr Watts-Dunton had exhausted the
praise with which he put me off ... then, if I was at all
insistent, extraordinary things would happen.... Loud
bells would ring all over the establishment. Housemaids
would rush in, their cap-strings floating behind, bearing
the orange envelopes of telegrams on silver salvers. And
Mr Watts-Dunton would start like a ship suddenly struck
by a gale, would tear open an envelope and exclaim
immediately:

'Sorry, me dear faller.... Extraordinarily sorry, me dear
faller.... Tallegram from Haslemere. From Lord Tenny-
son.... Have to go ... ah ... and correct his proofs at
once.... M'm, m'm, m'm.... Desolated to be unable
to be further delighted by most int'rustin' conversa....'
And he would have disappeared, the dimnesses swallowing
him up with improbable velocity....

When it wasn't Lord Tennyson, it would be Browning
... or Coventry Patmore or Lewis Morris....

And you are not to believe that Mr Watts-Dunton was
merely a toady. He was an extraordinarily assiduous and
skilful family lawyer and adviser as to investments and
solvent of brawls and poets' fallings out.... So that where
those poor Pre-Raphaelites would have been without him
there is no knowing.... His one novel ... *Aylwin* ... had
the largest sale ever enjoyed by any novel up to that date
and for decades after. It was what his friends called bilge,
and his innumerable poems seemed to be all devoted to
proving that he had once been kissed by a Romany lal ...
a sort of watered-down Isopel Berners.... But what else
could the poems and novels of the proprietor of the Pines,
Putney, be? ... And when reading his poems aloud to
Mr Swinburne, he would coyly hold his head on one side
as if the better to afford you the view of the spot on the
side of his jaw where the gipsy maiden had kissed him....
And I really believe one must have done so once.... But

he did save ever so many of those outrageous poet-painters from the workhouse or the gaol and kept as many more on this side of delirium tremens. . . .

On the less dramatic occasions when Mr Watts-Dunton really produced a cheque I would be invited to stay to lunch. . . . And owing to the increasing deafness of the two friends and of Mrs Mason the meals passed in ever deeper and deeper silence. . . . Mr Swinburne ate, lost in his dreams, with beside his plate an enormous Persian cat to whom he fed alternate forksful of food. Mr Watts-Dunton gobbled his meats with voracity. The cooking was exquisite, the wines quite impeccable—though Mr Swinburne touched none. Mrs Mason addressed inaudible remarks to the maids. . . .

At a given point she would catch the eye of non-existent ladies and rise stiffly. . . . Immediately, with an extremely jerky movement so rapid as to be almost imperceptible, Mr Swinburne would be on his toe-points, positively running to the door, his coat-tails flapping behind him. . . . It was the singular action of an extremely active man. At one moment he was sitting sunk in his chair; at the next he was on the points of his toes and in extraordinarily rapid motion. . . . Mrs Mason would be passing out of the doorway with a rigid inclination of the head to Mr Swinburne, who had opened the door for her; and slowly and meditatively the poet would regain his chair . . . with the litheness of a slow cat . . . and would begin to talk in long, wonderful monologues . . . about the *Bacchae* or the *Birds*.

A MR HARDY

I was keenly aware of a Mr Hardy who was a kind, small man, with a thin beard, in the background of London tea parties. . . and in the background of my mind . . . I remember very distinctly the tea party at which I was introduced to him by Mrs Lynn Lynton with her paralysing, pebble-blue eyes, behind gleaming spectacles. Mrs Lynn Lynton, also a novelist, was a Bad Woman, my dear. One of the Shrieking Sisterhood! And I could never have her glance bent on me from behind those glasses without being terrified at the fear that she might shriek . . . or be Bad. I think it was Rhoda Broughton who first scandalized London by giving her heroine a latchkey. But Mrs Lynn Lynton had done something as unspeakably wicked. . . . And I was a terribly proper young man.

So, out of a sort of kind of almost infantile paralysis— I must have been eighteen to the day—I found myself telling a very very kind, small, ageless, soft-voiced gentleman with a beard the name of my first book, which had been published a week before. And he put his head on one side and uttered, as if he were listening to himself, the syllables: 'Ow. . . . Ow. . . .'

I was petrified with horror . . . not because I thought he had gone mad or was being rude to me, but because he seemed to doom my book to irremediable failure. . . .

I do not believe I have ever mentioned the name of one of my own books in my own print . . . at least I hope I have been too much of a little gentleman ever to have done so. But I do not see how I can here avoid mentioning that my first book was called *The Brown Owl* and that it was only a fairy tale . . . I will add that the publisher —for whom Mr Edward Garnett was literary adviser— paid me ten pounds for it and that it sold many thousands more copies than any other book I ever wrote . . . and keeps on selling to this day.

And on that day I had not got over the queer feeling of having had a book published . . . I hadn't wanted to have a book published. I hadn't tried to get it published. My grandfather had, as it were, ordered Mr Garnett to get it published. . . . I can to this day hear my grandfather's voice saying to Mr Garnett, who was sitting to him on a model's throne:

'Fordie has written a book, too.... Go and get your book, Fordie!'... and the manuscript at the end of Mr Garnett's very thin wrist disappearing into his capacious pocket.... And my mother let me have ten shillings of the money paid by Mr Garnett's employer.... And that I thought authorship was on the whole a mug's game and concealed as well as I could from my young associates the fact that I was an Author. I should have told you that that was my attitude and should have believed it. My ambition in those days was to be an Army Officer!

And then suddenly, in Mrs Lynn Lynton's dim, wicked drawing-room, in face of this kind, bearded gentleman, I was filled with consternation and grief. Because it was plain that he considered that the vowel sounds of the title of my book were ugly and that, I supposed, would mean that the book could not succeed. So I made the discovery that I—but tremendously!—wished that the book should succeed ... even though I knew that if the book should succeed it would for ever damn my chances as one of Her Majesty's officers....

And I could feel Mr Hardy feeling the consternation and grief that had come up in me, because he suddenly said in a voice that was certainly meant to be consolatory:

'But of course you meant to be onomatopoeic. Ow—ow—representing the lamenting voices of owls.... Like the repeated double O's of the opening of the Second Book of *The Aeneid*....'

I was struck as dumb as a stuck pig. I could not get out a word whilst he went on talking cheerfully. He told me some anecdotes of the brown owl and then remarked that it might perhaps have been better if, supposing I had wanted to represent in my title the cry of the brown owl, instead of two 'ow' sounds I could have found two 'oo's.'.... And he reflected and tried over the sound of 'the brooding coots' and 'the muted lutes....'

And then he said, as if miraculously to my easement:

'But of course you're quite right.... One shouldn't talk of one's books at tea parties.... Drop in at Max Gate when you are passing and we'll talk about it all in peace. . . .'

Marvellously kind . . . and leaving me still with a new emotional qualm of horror. . . . Yes, I was horrified . . . because I had let that kind gentleman go away thinking that my book was about birds . . . whereas it was about Princesses and Princes and magicians and such twaddle. . . . I had written it to amuse my sister Juliet. . . . So I ran home and wrote him a long letter telling him that the book was not about birds and begging his pardon in several distinct ways. . . .

FORD MADOX BROWN

I

MADOX BROWN has been dead for twenty years now, or getting on for that. I would not say that the happiest days of my life were those that I spent in his studio, for I have spent in my life days as happy since then; but I will say that Madox Brown was the finest man I ever knew. He had his irascibilities, his fits of passion when, tossing his white head, his mane of hair would fly all over his face, and when he would blaspheme impressively after the manner of our great-grandfathers. And in these fits of temper he would frequently say the most unjust things. But I think that he was never either unjust or ungenerous in cold blood, and I am quite sure that envy had no part at all in his nature. Like Rossetti and like William Morris, in his very rages he was nearest to generosities. He would rage over an injustice to someone else to the point of being bitterly unjust to the oppressor. I do not think that I would care to live my life over again—I have had days that I would not again face for a good deal—but I would give very much of what I possess to be able, having still such causes for satisfaction as I now have in life, to be able to live once more some of those old evenings in the studio.

The lights would be lit, the fire would glow between the red tiles; my grandfather would sit with his glass of weak whisky-and-water in his hand, and would talk for hours. He had anecdotes more lavish and more picturesque than any man I ever knew. He would talk of Beau Brummel, who had been British Consul at Calais when Madox Brown was born there, of Paxton who built the Crystal Palace, and of the mysterious Duke of Portland who lived underground, but who, meeting Madox Brown in Baker Street outside Druce's, and hearing that Madox Brown suffered from gout, presented him with a large quantity of colchicum grown at Welbeck. . . .

Well, I would sit there on the other side of the rustling fire, listening, and he would revive the splendid ghosts of Pre-Raphaelites, going back to Cornelius and Overbeck and to Baron Leys and Baron Wappers, who sought him first to paint in the romantic grand manner. He would talk on. Then Mr William Rossetti would come in from next door but one, and they would begin to talk of Shelley and Browning and Mazzini and Napoleon III, and Mr Rossetti, sitting in front of the fire, would sink his head nearer and nearer the flames. His right leg would be crossed over his left knee, and, as his head went down, so, of necessity, his right foot would come up and out. It would approach nearer and nearer to the fire-irons which stood at the end of the fender. The tranquil talk would continue. Presently the foot would touch the fire-irons and down they would go into the fender with a tremendous clatter of iron. Madox Brown, half dozing in the firelight, would start and spill some of his whisky. I would replace the fire-irons in their stand.

The talk would continue, Mr Rossetti beginning again to sink his head towards the fire, and explaining that, as he was not only bald but an Italian, he liked to have his head warmed. Presently, bang! would go the fire-irons again. Madox Brown would lose some more whisky and would exclaim:

'Really, William!'

Mr Rossetti would say:

'I am very sorry, Brown.'

I would replace the fire-irons again, and the talk would continue. And then for the third time the fire-irons would go down. Madox Brown would hastily drink what little whisky remained to him, and jumping to his feet would shout:

'God damn and blast you, William, can't you be more careful?'

To which his son-in-law, always the most utterly calm of men, would reply:

'Really, Brown, your emotion appears to be excessive. If Fordie would leave the fire-irons lying in the fender there would be no occasion for them to fall.'

The walls were covered with gilded leather; all the doors were painted dark green; the room was very long, and partly filled by the great picture that was never to be finished, and, all in shadow, in the distant corner was the table covered with bits of string, curtain knobs, horseshoes, and odds and ends of iron and wood.

II

It was a few days after this, in the evening, that Madox Brown, painting at his huge picture, pointed to the top of the frame that already surrounded the canvas. Upon the top was inscribed 'Ford Madox Brown,' and on the bottom, *Wycliffe on his Trial before John of Gaunt. Presented to the National Gallery by a Committee of Admirers of the Artist.* In this way the 'X' of Madox Brown came exactly over the centre of the picture. It was Madox Brown's practice to begin a painting by putting in the eyes of the central figure. This, he considered, gave him the requisite strength of tone that would be applied to the whole canvas. And indeed I believe that, once he had painted in those eyes, he never in any picture altered them, however much he might alter the picture itself. He used them, as it were, to work up to. Having painted in those eyes he would begin at the top left-hand corner of the canvas, and would go on painting downwards in a nearly straight line until the picture was finished. He would of course have made a great number of studies before commencing the picture itself. Usually there was an exceedingly minute and conscientious pencil-drawing, then a large charcoal cartoon, and after that, for the sake of the colour scheme, a version in water-colour, in pastels, and generally one in oil. In the case of the Manchester frescoes almost every one was preceded by a small version painted in oils upon a panel, and this was the case with the large Wycliffe.

On this, the last evening of his life, Madox Brown pointed with his brush to the 'X' of his name. Below it, on the left-hand side the picture was completely filled in: on the right it was completely blank—a waste of slightly yellow canvas that gleamed in the dusky studio. He said:

'You see I have got to that "X." I am glad of it, for half the picture is done and it feels as if I were going home.'

Those, I think, were his last words. He laid his brushes upon his painting cabinet, scraped his palette of all mixed paints, laid his palette upon his brushes and his spectacles upon his palette. He took off the biretta that he always wore when he was painting—he must have worn such a biretta for upwards of half a century—ever since he had been a French student. And so having arrived at his end-of-the-day routine which he had followed for innumerable years, he went upstairs to bed. He probably read a little of the *Mystères de Paris*, and died in his sleep, the picture with its inscriptions remaining downstairs, a little ironic, a little pathetic, and unfinished.

MR HOWELL AND MR ROSSETTI

Rossetti wanted to fill his house with anything that was odd, Chinese, or sparkling. If there was something gruesome about it, he liked it all the better. Thus at his death, two marauders, out of the shady crew that victimized him and one honest man, each became possessed of the dark lantern used by Eugene Aram. I mean to say that quite lately there were in the market three dark lanterns each of which was supposed to have come from Rossetti's house at his death, only one of which had been bought with honest money at Rossetti's sale. Even this one may not have been the relic of the murderer which Rossetti had purchased with immense delight. He bought in fact just anything or everything that amused him or tickled his fancy, without the least idea of making his house resemble anything but an old curiosity shop.

This collection was rendered still more odd by the eccentricities of Mr Charles Augustus Howell, an extraordinary personage who ought to have a volume all to himself. There was nothing in an odd-jobbing way that Mr Howell was not up to. He supported his family for some time by using a diving bell to recover treasure from a lost galleon off the coast of Portugal, of which country he appears to have been a native. He became Ruskin's secretary and he had a shop in which he combined the framing and the forging of masterpieces. He conducted the most remarkable of dealers' swindles with the most consummate ease and grace, doing it indeed so lovably that when his misdeeds were discovered he became only more beloved. Such a character would obviously appeal to Rossetti, and as, at one period of his career, Rossetti's income ran well into five figures, whilst he threw gold out of all the windows and doors, it is obvious that such a character as Rossetti's must have appealed very strongly to Mr Charles Augustus Howell. The stories of him are endless. At one time whilst Rossetti was collecting chinoiseries, Howell happened to have in his possession a nearly priceless set of Chinese tea-things. These he promptly proceeded to have duplicated at his establishment, where forging was carried on more wonderfully than seems possible. This forgery he proceeded to get one of his concealed agents to sell to Rossetti for an enormously high figure. Coming to tea with the poet-artist on the next day, he remarked to Rossetti:

9*

'Hallo, Gabriel, where did you get those clumsy imitations?'

Rossetti of course was filled with consternation, whereupon Howell remarked comfortingly: 'Oh, it's all right, old chap, I've got the originals, which I'll let you have for an old song.'

And eventually, he sold the originals to Rossetti for a figure very considerably over that at which Rossetti had bought the forgeries. Howell was then permitted to take away the forgeries as of no value, and Rossetti was left with the originals. Howell, however, was for some time afterwards more than usually assiduous in visiting the painter-poet. At each visit he brought one of the forged cups in his pocket and whilst Rossetti's back was turned he substituted the forgery for one of the genuine cups which he took away in his pocket. At the end of the series of visits, therefore, Rossetti once more possessed the copies and Howell the genuine set which he sold, I believe, to M. Tissot.

A SETTLEMENT OF ALIENS

Winchelsea stands on a long bluff, in shape like that of Gibraltar. Two miles of marsh separate it from Rye. Once it was sea where the Marsh now is: one day it will be so again. When it was sea all the navies of England could ride in that harbour. And the Five Ports and the two Antient Towns provided all the navies of the King of England. As against certain privileges. A Baron of the Cinque Ports can still drive through all toll-gates without payment and sell in all markets toll-free.

In the face of the cliff that Winchelsea turns to Rye there is a spring forming a dip—St Leonard's Well, or the Wishing Well. The saying is that once you have drunk of those dark waters you will never rest till you drink again.

I have seen—indeed I have induced them to it—Henry James, Stephen Crane, and W. H. Hudson drink there from the hollows of their hands. So did Conrad. They are all dead now.

It was perhaps those waters that induced their frequentations of those two towns. But indeed there were sufficient other inducements. Historic patina covers their buildings more deeply than any others, in England at least. Indeed, I know of no places save for Paris, where memories seem so thick on every stone. The climate too is very mild. There is practically no day throughout the year on which a proper man cannot eat his meals under a south wall out of doors. Then, it is near France. On most days you can see the French cliffs. Once, by an effect of mirage, the city of Boulogne was brought so near to Hastings which is next door to Rye, that the promenaders on the parade of the English town could discern the faces of the tourists inspecting the column of Napoleon on the Boulogne sward over the sea. Napoleon erected that to celebrate his invasion of England. That was as near as anything of his ever got to the coasts of the Five Ports.

At any rate it is an infectious and holding neighbourhood. Once you go there you are apt there to stay. Or you will see in memory, the old walled towns, the red roofs, the grey stones, the country sweeping back in steps from the Channel to the North Downs, the great stretch of the Romney Marsh running out to Dungeness. In the Middle Ages they used to say: 'These be the four quarters of the world: Europe, Asia, Africa, and the Romney Marsh.' But that was before Columbus committed his indiscretion. Hendrik Hudson drew many of his sailors from Rye town. A Rye man was the first European to lose his life by an arrow, in Manhattan; on the shores of the Hudson, I should imagine, beneath where Grant's grave is. . . .

Some years ago my friend Mr H. G. Wells wrote to the papers to say that for many years he was conscious of a ring of foreign conspirators plotting against British letters at no great distance from his residence, Spade House,

Sandgate.... For indeed, those four men—three Americans and one Pole—lit in those days in England a beacon that posterity shall not easily die. You have only got to consider how empty, how lacking a nucleus, English literature would to-day be if they had never lived, to see how discerning were Mr Wells' views of that foreign penetration at the most vulnerable point of England's shores.

At that date Henry James was clean-shaven. As clean-shavenness was then comparatively rare he had in his relatively quiet moments the air of a divine; when, which was more frequent, he was animated, he was nearly always humorous and screwed his sensitive lips into amused or sardonic lines. Then he was like a comedian. His skin was dark, his face very clear cut, his brow domed and bare. His eyes were singularly penetrating, dark and a little prominent. On their account he was regarded by the neighbouring poor as having the qualities of a Wise Man—a sorcerer. My servants used to say: 'It always gives me a turn to open the door for Mr James. His eyes seems to look you through to the very back-bone.'

His vitality was amazing. You might put it that he was very seldom still and almost never silent. Occasionally when he desired information and you were giving him what he wanted he would sit gazing at you with his head leaning back against his grandfather's chair. But almost immediately he would be off with comment and elucidation—or with more questions accompanied by gestures, raising of the eyebrows and the humorous twisting of his lips. His peculiarities were carefully thought out by himself. A distinguished man in the 'fifties must have peculiarities if he has a strong personality. His conversation used to contain a great many compliments to his interlocutor, male or female. They were the current coin of his conversation, learned in France and having no real significance but the fact that they were agreeable. Every woman from the Lady Maude Warrender on the hill to Meary Walker in the marshes was 'dear lady'; every man, 'my dear fellow.' If you did or produced anything it was always admirable: 'Your admirable verses, your admirable still lifes, tea-cakes, knowledge of stock-exchange operations, market gardening.' It was agreeable when you were used to it but many people it bewildered or repelled because of a supposed insincerity. Until you know a person well it is perhaps not ethically better to say to him or her: '*Muy hermosa senora beso los manos de usted,*' than to employ a universal 'buddy' for social contacts. But it is not insincere.

On the other hand if he liked or were intimate with you his manner changed at once. You would not lack for censure, criticism, or exhortations along with exactly calculated praise. He liked to live with people of leisure who were intellectually no wasters of time. At times he was unreasonably cruel—and that to the point of vindictiveness when his nerves were set on edge. I remember him at a tea-party given by one of his most gentle and modest admirers. He was talking to the young man's equally gentle, modest, and adoring wife. The young man interrupted him by several times offering him sugar, tea-cakes, cigars. The things that he at last spat out to that young man I will not repeat. He indicted his manners, his hospitality, his dwelling, his work, with a cold fury in voice and eyes.

I was once walking with him and Mr John Galsworthy along the Rye Road to Winchelsea. His dachshund, Maximilian, ran sheep, so, not to curtail the animal's exercise, the Master had provided it with a leash at least ten yards long. Mr Galsworthy and I walked one on each side of James listening obediently whilst he talked. In order to round off an immense sentence the great man halted, just under Winchelsea Hill beneath the windows of acquaintances of us all. He planted his stick firmly into the ground and went on and on and on. Maximilian passed between our six legs again and again, threading his leash behind him. Mr Galsworthy and I stood silent. In any case we must have resembled the *Laocoon*, but when

Maximilian had finished the resemblance must have been overwhelming. The Master finished his reflections, attempted to hurry on, found that impossible. Then we liberated ourselves with difficulty. He turned on me, his eyes fairly blazing, lifting his cane on high and slamming it into the ground:

'H...' he exclaimed, 'you are painfully young, but at no more than the age to which you have attained, the playing of such tricks is an imbecility! An im...be...cility!'

The politenesses of Conrad to James and of James to Conrad were of the most impressive kind. Even if they had been addressing each other from the tribune of the Académie Française their phrases could not have been more elaborate or delivered more *ore rotundo*. James always addressed Conrad as '*Mon cher confrère*,' Conrad almost bleated with the peculiar tone that the Marseillaise get into their compliments '*Mon cher Maître*.'... Every thirty seconds! When James spoke of me to Conrad he always said: '*Votre ami, le jeune homme modeste*.' They always spoke French together, James using an admirably pronounced, correct, and rather stilted idiom such as prevailed in Paris of the 'seventies. Conrad spoke with extraordinary speed, fluency, and some incomprehensibility, a meridional French with as strong a Southern accent as that of garlic in *aioli*.... I speak French with a strong British accent and much too correctly. When I was a boy my grandfather who was French by birth and had a strong French tinge to his English used to say to me: 'Fordie, you must speak French with absolute correctness and without slang which would be an affectation. But with the strongest possible British accent to show that you are an English gentleman.'

We talked in those days, with those distinctions of language, for many hours on end. Or rather, I listened whilst they talked.

Conrad had the most unbounded, the most generous, and the most understanding admiration for the Master's work but he did not much like James personally. I imagine that was because at bottom James was a New Englander *pur sang*, though he was actually born in New York. James on the other hand liked neither Conrad nor his work very much, mostly, I imagine, because at bottom Conrad was a Pole, a Roman Catholic and Romantic and Slav pessimist. It was hardly to be expected that James should like, say, *Lord Jim*, for, though that may less appear to-day, the technique of Conrad's work was then singularly revolutionary. James on the other hand never made fun of Conrad in private. Conrad was never for him 'poor dear old' as were Flaubert, Mrs Humphry Ward, Meredith, Hardy, or Sir Edmund Gosse. He once expressed to me as regards Conrad something like an immense respect for his character and achievements. I cannot remember his exact words, but they were something to the effect that Conrad's works impressed him very disagreeably, but he could find no technical fault or awkwardness about them. So that since so many men whose judgment he affected regarded Conrad even then as a great master he must not be taken as uttering any literary censure. . . .

The Conrad of those days was Romance. He was dark, black bearded, passionate in the extreme and at every minute; rather small but very broad shouldered and long in the arm. Speaking English he had so strong a French accent that few who did not know him well could understand him at first. His gestures were profuse and continuous, his politenesses Oriental and at times almost servile. Like James he would address a Society lady, if he ever met one, or an old woman in the lane, or his own servants, or the ostler at an inn, or myself who was for many years little more than his cook, slut, and butler in literary matters, or Sir Sidney Colvin, or Sir Edmund Gosse, all with the same profusion of endearing adjectives. On the other hand his furies would be sudden, violent, blasting, and incomprehensible to his victim. At one of my afternoon parties in London he objurgated the unfortunate Charles Lewis Hind—a thin, slightly stuttering nervous, dark fellow who was noted as a critic, mostly of paintings. Hind in a perfectly sincere mood had congratulated him because his name was on all the hoardings in London. Conrad's *Nostromo* was then being serialized in a journal that gave the fact unusual prominence in its advertisements.

Conrad on the other hand despised the journal, and himself more for letting his work appear in it. His hatred of the publicity was as real as if it were an outrage on the honour of his family. From the windows of my house his name was visible on a hoarding that some house-breakers had erected—visible in letters three feet long. This had driven him nearly mad and he had really taken the congratulations of Mr Hind as gloatings over his bitter poverty. Mr Hind had a sardonic manner and spoke with a rictus; bitter and dreadfully harassing poverty alone had driven Conrad, mercilessly, to consent to that degradation of his art.

In the event, next day Conrad was very ill with mortification and I had to write the part of the serial that remained to make up the weekly instalment. Our life was like that. That manuscript of mine is in the hands of an American collector.*

Otherwise he was the most marvellous raconteur in the world. There was no country he could not make you see when he talked, from Poland to the palms of Palembang. He suffered at that time and till towards the end of his life from agonies of poverty. He was terribly concerned for the material future of his family to whom he was almost unbelievably attached. Crane and Hudson he really loved personally. His admiration for their works was unbounded. When their books came it was as if he bounded into them like a schoolboy running from the school door. I do not think he took much real stock in other writers of English. He would utter elaborate politenesses to them if he met them.

But you could always tell when he really admired work. It would manifest itself in two ways. You would be read-

* The long instalment of *Nostromo* in Ford's handwriting without any corrections by Conrad is now in Yale University Library.

ing at one end of the room and he at the other. It would be a new book he was reading—or perhaps a Flaubert, a Turgenev, or a Maupassant. He would begin to groan and roll about on the couch where he was extended. After a time he would say:

'What is the use? I ask you what is the use of writing? When this fellow can write like this. There's no room for us.' He would go on groaning. Then he would, after a time, spring up, holding his book. 'Listen to this!' he would exclaim in sheer joy; laughing with it as if with his whole body; 'By God,' he would cry out, 'There was never anything like this.' And he would read out a phrase of Crane's 'The waves were barbarous and abrupt'; or a short passage of Hudson in which he shows you dandelion globes, when you are lying on your back on Lewes Downs, globes illuminated by the sun against the blue sky, in millions, for miles up into the blue. Or he would close a book by Henry James, sigh deeply and say: 'I don't know how the Old Man does it. There's nothing he does not know; there's nothing he can't do. That's what it is when you have been privileged to go about with Turgenev.'

Hudson immensely admired Conrad personally. He was very lean, *very* tall, high-boned, long-limbed, grey. He was slow in his motions. You have to be if you are a field naturalist. His head was smallish for his great frame, but as if chiselled by the wind as rocks are; his cheeks weather-beaten. His eyes were small and keen, usually a little closed as if he were looking up along a strong wind. His voice was very gentle, soft as a rule, sometimes a little high and reedy, his accent neither English nor American, but very scrupulous. He had a little, short, pointed, grey hidalgo's beard and a heavy grey moustache. He was all gentleness and infinite patience. I have been with him in circumstances of ill-natured companionship and querulousness in which his patience was unending. He would stroll along, swinging his shoulders, stooping a little, mostly silent, occasionally putting in a word of dissent. To show that he was paying attention. He suggested, the immensely long fellow, a man holding in his hand a frightened bird, but making his examination with such gentleness that the bird's little heart would soon cease to beat fast. If he stood against an old grey wall in a field he was so grey that he would be almost invisible from a few yards away unless you looked specially for him.

He knew on the surface little about books. He would say again and again, indignantly: 'I am no writer. I am a naturalist.' He looked at books from afar. It was perhaps long-sightedness but it gave the idea that he was mentally aloof. He would stand up, holding *Heart of Darkness* and say 'Well, the sea is all right. The trees are all right. Yes, not so bad. No doubt he's a master.' James personally a little alarmed him. Hudson was used to high society, moving in aloof realms that are usually closed to imaginative writers. They were then open to almost all Americans, because they committed you to nothing socially. The Greys of Fallodon loved Hudson because he loved birds. So he would look at James enigmatically, breathing rather uncertainly through his nose. James was a Society figure all right—but a little too flamboyant. Like an unusual species of a familiar genus. The early works of James in their first versions Hudson liked and he was ready to acknowledge that the Old Man was the Master of us all. Old Man means 'captain' on a ship, a colonel in a regiment, a head foreman in a gang of stevedores, a master shepherd on a farm.

Crane was the most beautiful spirit I have ever known. He was small, frail, energetic, at times virulent. He was full of phantasies and fantasticisms. He would fly at and deny every statement before it was out of your mouth. He wore breeches, riding leggings, spurs, a cowboy's shirt, and there was always a gun near him in the mediaeval building that he inhabited seven miles from Winchelsea. In that ancient edifice he would swat flies with precision and satisfaction with the bead-sight of his gun. He proclaimed all day long that he had no use for corner lots nor battlefields, but he got his death in a corner, on the most

momentous of all battlefields for Anglo-Saxons. Brede
Manor saw the encampment of Harold before Hastings.

He was an American, pure blooded, and of ostentatious
manners when he wanted to be. He used to declare at one
time that he was the son of an uptown New York bishop,
at another, that he had been born in the Bowery and there
dragged up. At one moment his voice would be harsh, like
a raven's, uttering phrases like: 'I'm a fly-guy that's wise
to the all-night push,' if he wanted to be taken for a
Bowery tough, or 'He was a mangy, sheep-stealing coyote'
if he desired to be thought of cowboy ancestry. At other
times he would talk rather low in very selected English.
That was all boyishness.

But he was honourable, physically brave, infinitely hope-
ful, generous, charitable to excess, observant beyond belief,
morally courageous, of unswerving loyalty, a beautiful poet
—and of untiring industry. With his physical frailty, his
idealism, his love of freedom and of truth he seemed to me
to be like Shelley. His eyes with their long fringes of
lashes were almost incredibly beautiful—and as if vengeful.
Of his infinite industry he had need.

It was delightful to go to Brede Place, because Steevie
was there, but nothing was more depressing than to drive
down into the hollow. In the Middle Ages they built in
bottoms to be near water and Brede, though mostly an
Elizabethan building, in the form of an E out of compli-
ment to Great Eliza, was twelfth-century in site. The
sunlight penetrated, pale, like a blight into that damp
depression. The great house was haunted. It had stood
empty for half a century, the rendezvous of smugglers. On
the green banks played fatherless children—and number-
less parasites. Crane never forgot a friend, even if it were
merely a fellow who had passed a wet night with him
under an arch. His wife was minded to be a mediaeval
chatelaine. A barrel of beer and a baron of beef stood
waiting in the rear hall for every hobo that might pass that
way. The house was a nightmare of misplaced hospitality,

of lugubrious dissipation in which Crane himself had no part. Grub Street and Greenwich Village did.

The effect on James of poor Steevie was devastating. Crane rode about the countryside on one of two immense coach-horses that he possessed. On their rawboned carcases his frail figure looked infinitely tiny and forlorn. At times he would rein up before the Old Man's door and going in would tell the Master's titled guests that he was a fly-guy that was wise to all the all-night pushes of the world. The Master's titled guests liked it. It was, they thought, characteristic of Americans. If the ~~martin had been afluted they would~~ have thought themselves confronted with someone from Hollywood. James winced and found it unbearable.

Steevie he stood and would have stood a great deal more from. The boy for him was always: 'My young compatriot of genius.' But he would explain his wincings to English people by: 'It's as if . . . oh dear lady it's as if you should find in a staid drawing-room on Beacon Hill or Washington Square or at an intimate reception at an Embassy at Washington a Cockney—oh, I admit of the greatest genius —but a Cockney, still, Costermonger from Whitechapel. And, oh heavens, received, surrounded, and adulated . . . by, ah, the choicest, the loveliest, the most sympathetic, and, ah, the most ornamental. . . .'

And the joke—or, for the Old Man the tragedy—was that Crane assumed his Bowery cloak for the sole purpose of teasing the Master. In much the same way, taking me for a Pre-Raphaelite poet, at the beginning of our friendship, he would be for ever harshly denouncing those who paid special prices for antiquities. To Conrad or to Hudson, on the other hand, he spoke and behaved as a reasoning and perceptive human being.

And indeed the native beauty of his nature penetrated sufficiently to the Old Man himself. I never heard James say anything intimately damaging of Crane, and I do not believe he ever said anything of that sort to other people. But what made the situation really excruciating to James was the raids made by Crane's parasites on Lamb House. No doors could keep them out, nor no butler. They made hideous the still levels of the garden with their cachinations, they poked the Old Man in the ribs before his servants, caricatured his speeches before his guests, and extracted from him loans that were almost never refused. There were times when he would hang about in the country outside Rye Walls rather than make such an encounter.

The final tragedy of poor Steevie did not find him wanting. It was tragedy. The sunlight fell blighted into that hollow, the spectres waved their draped arms of mist, the parasites howled and belched on the banks at Brede. That was horrible. But much more horrible was the sight of Crane at his labours. They took place in a room in the centre bar of the E of the Place, over the arched entry. Here Crane would sit writing, hour after hour and day after day, racked with the anxiety that he would not be able to keep going with his pen alone all that fantastic crew. His writing was tiny: he used great sheets of paper. To see him begin at the top of the sheet with his tiny words was agonizing; to see him finish a page filled you with concern. It meant the beginning of one more page, and so till his death. Death came slowly, but Brede was a sure death trap to the tuberculous.

Then James's agonies began. He suffered infinitely for that dying boy. I would walk with him for hours over the Marsh trying to divert his thoughts. But he would talk on and on. He was for ever considering devices for Crane's comfort. Once he telegraphed to Wanamaker's for a whole collection of New England delicacies from pumpkin pie to apple butter and sausage meat and clams and soft shell crabs and mincemeat and . . . everything thinkable, so that the poor lad should know once more and finally those fierce joys. Then new perplexities devastated him. Perhaps the taste of those far off meats might cause Steevie to be homesick and so hasten his end. He wavered backwards and forwards between the alternatives beneath the grey walls of Rye Town. He was not himself for many days after Crane's death.

So the first of those four men to die was the youngest. Taken altogether they were, those four, all gods for me. They formed, when I was a boy, my sure hope in the eternity of good letters. They do still. Long ago the greatest pride of my life used to be that Crane once wrote of me to a friend; I had presumably upset him by some want of Oriental deference:

'You must not mind Hueffer, that is his way. He patronises me; he patronises Mr Conrad; he patronises Mr James. When he goes to Heaven he will patronise God Almighty. But God Almighty will get used to it, for Hueffer is all right.'

And the words are my greatest pride after so many years.

They are now all dead, a fact which seems to me incredible still. For me they were the greatest influence on the literature that has followed after them that has yet been vouchsafed to that literature. That fourfold tradition will not soon part. To that tradition I will one day return. For the moment I have been trying to make them live again in your eyes. . . . 'It is above all to make you see.'

THE OLD MAN

I daresay, if we could only perceive it, Life has a pattern. I don't mean that of birth, apogee, and death, but a woven symbolism of its own. The Pattern in the Carpet, Henry James called it—and that he saw something of the sort was no doubt the secret of his magic. But, though I walked with and listened to the Master day after day, I remember only one occasion on which he made a remark that was a revelation of his own aims and methods. . . . For the rest, our intercourse resolved itself into my listening silently and wondering unceasingly at his observation of the littlest things of life.

'Are you acquainted,' he would begin, as we strolled under the gateway down Winchelsea Hill towards Rye. . . . Ellen Terry would wave a gracious hand from her garden above the old Tower, the leash of Maximilian would require several readjustments, and the dog himself a great many *sotto voce* admonitions as to his expensive habit of chasing sheep into dykes. 'Are you acquainted,' the Master would begin again, 'with the terrible words. . . .'

A higgler, on a cart burdened with crates of live poultry, would pass us. The Master would drive the point of his cane into the roadway. 'Now *that* man!' he would exclaim. And he would break off to say what hideous, what appalling, what bewildering, what engrossing, Affairs were going on all round us in the little white cottages and farms that we could see, dotting Playden Hill and the Marsh to the verge of the great horizon. 'Terrible things!' he would say. 'Appalling!' . . . 'Now that man who just passed us. . . .' And then he would dig his stick into the road again and hurry forward, like the White Queen escaping from disaster, dropping over his shoulder the words: 'But that probably would not interest you. . . .'

I don't know what he thought *would* interest me!

So he would finish his sentence before the door above the high steps of Lamb House:

'Are you acquainted with the terrible, the devastating words, if I may call them so, the fiat of Doom: "I don't know if you know, sir?" As when the housemaid comes into your bedroom in the morning and says: "I don't know if you know, sir, that the bath has fallen through the kitchen ceiling." '

It was held in Rye that he practised black magic behind the high walls of Lamb House. . . .

I think I will, after reflection, lay claim to a very considerable degree of intimacy with Henry James. It was a winter, and a wholly non-literary intimacy. That is to say, during the summers we saw little of each other. He had his friends, and I mine. He was too often expecting 'my friend Lady Maude,' or some orthodox critic to tea, and I, modern poets whom he could not abide. Occasionally, even during the summer, he would send from Rye to Winchelsea, a distance of two miles, telegrams such as the following which I transcribe:

'To Ford Madox Hueffer, Esq.,
'The Bungalow, Winchelsea, near Rye, Sussex.
     'May I bring four American ladies, of whom one

                         'Yours sincerely,
                              'Henry James.'

And he would come.

But in the winters, when London visitors were scarce, he would come to tea every other day with almost exact regularity, and I would walk back with him to Rye. On the alternate days I would have tea with him and he would walk back to Winchelsea, in all weathers, across the wind-swept marshes. That was his daily, four miles, constitutional.

But it was, as I have said, an almost purely non-literary intimacy. I could, I think, put down on one page all that he ever said to me of books—and, although I used, out of respect, to send him an occasional book of my own on publication, and he an occasional book of his to me, he never said a word to me about my writings and I do not remember ever having done more than thank him in letters for his volume of the moment. I remember his saying of *Romance* that it was an immense English Plum Cake which he kept at his bedside for a fortnight and of which he ate a nightly slice.

He would, if he never talked of books, frequently talk of the personalities of their writers—not infrequently in terms of shuddering at their social excess, much as he shuddered at contact with Crane. He expressed intense dislike for Flaubert who 'opened his own door in his dressing-gown' and he related, not infrequently, unrepeat-able stories of the *ménages* of Maupassant—but he much preferred Maupassant to 'poor dear old Flaubert.' Of Turgenev's appearance, personality and habits, he would talk with great tenderness of expression—he called him nearly always 'the beautiful Russian genius,' and would tell stories of Turgenev's charming attentions to his peasant mistresses. He liked, in fact, persons who were suave when you met them—and I daresay that his pre-ference of that sort coloured his literary tastes. He pre-ferred Maupassant to Flaubert because Maupassant was *homme du monde*—or at any rate had *femmes du monde* for his mistresses; and he preferred Turgenev to either because Turgenev was a quiet aristocrat and invalid of the German Bathing Towns, to the finger-tips. And he liked—he used to say so—people who treated him with deep respect.

Flaubert he hated with a lasting, deep rancour. Flaubert had once abused him unmercifully—over a point in the style of Prosper Merimée, of all people in the world. You may read about it in the *Correspondence* of Flaubert, and James himself referred to that occasion several times. It seemed to make it all the worse that, just before the outbreak, Flaubert should have opened the front door of his flat to Turgenev and James, in his dressing-gown.

Myself, I suppose he must have liked, because I treated him with deep respect, had a low voice—appeared in short, a *jeune homme modeste*. Occasionally he would burst out at me with furious irritation—as if I had been a stupid nephew. This would be particularly the case if I ventured to have any opinions about the United States —which, at that date, I had visited much more lately than he had. I remember one occasion very vividly—the place, beside one of the patches of thorn on the Rye road, and his aspect, the brown face with the dark eyes rolling in the whites, the compact, strong figure, the stick raised so as to be dug violently into the road. He had been talk-ing two days before of the provincialism of Washington in the 'sixties. He said that when one descended the steps of the Capitol in those days *on trébuchait sur des vaches* —one stumbled over cows, as if on a village green. Two days later, I don't know why—I happened to return to the subject of the provincialism of Washington in the 'sixties. He stopped as if I had hit him and, with the coldly infuriated tone of a country squire whose patriotism had been outraged, exclaimed:

'Don't talk such *damnable* nonsense!' He really shouted these words with a male fury. And when, slightly outraged myself I returned to the charge with his own *trébuchait sur des vaches,* he exclaimed: 'I should not have thought you would have wanted to display such ignorance,' and hurried off along the road.

I do not suppose that this was as unreasonable a manifestation of patriotism as it appears. No doubt he imagined me incapable of distinguishing between material and cultural poverties and I am fairly sure that, at the bottom of his mind lay the idea that in Washington of the 'sixties there had been some singularly good cosmopolitan and diplomatic conversation and society, whatever the cows might have done outside the Capitol. Indeed I know that towards the end of his life, he came to think that the society of early, self-conscious New England, with its circumscribed horizon and want of exterior decoration or furnishings, was a spiritually finer thing than the mannered Europeanism that had so taken him to its bosom. As these years went on, more and more, with a sort of trepidation, he hovered round the idea of a return to the American Scene. When I first knew him you could have imagined no oak more firmly planted in European soil. But, little by little, when he talked about America there would come into his tones a slight tremulousness that grew with the months. I remember, once he went to see some friends— Mrs and Miss Lafarge, I think—off to New York from Tilbury Dock. He came back singularly excited, bringing out a great many unusually uncompleted sentences. He had gone over the liner: 'And once aboard the lugger. . . .

And if.... Say a toothbrush.... And circular notes....
And something for the night....' All this with a sort of
diffident shamefacedness.

I fancy that his mannerisms—his involutions, whether
in speech or in writing, were due to a settled conviction
that, neither in his public nor in his acquaintance, would
he ever find anyone who would not need talking down to.
The desire of the Artist, of the creative writer, is that his
words and his 'scenes' shall suggest—of course with pre-
cision—far more than they actually express or project.
But, having found that his limpidities, from *Daisy Miller*
to *The Real Thing*, not only suggested less than he desired,
but carried suggestions entirely unmeant, he gave up the
attempt at Impressionism of that type—as if his audiences
had tired him out. So he talked down to us, explaining and
explaining, the ramifications of his mind. He was aiming
at explicitness, never at obscurities—as if he were talking
to children.

At any rate, then, he had none of that provincialism of
the literary mind which must forever be dragging in
allusions to some book or local custom. If he found it
necessary to allude to one or the other he explained them
and their provenance. In that you saw that he had learned
in the same school as Conrad and Stephen Crane. And
indeed he had.

It has always seemed to me inscrutable that he should
have been so frequently damned for his depicting only
one phase of life; as if it were his fault that he was not
also Conrad, to write of the sea, or Crane, to project the
life of the New York slums. The Old Man knew consum-
mately one form of life; to that he restricted himself. I
have heard him talk with extreme exactness and insight
of the life of the poor—at any rate of the agricultural
poor, for I do not remember ever to have heard him
discuss industrialism. But he knew that he did not know
enough to treat of farm labourers in his writing. So that,
mostly, when he discoursed of these matters he put his

observations in the form of question: 'Didn't I agree to this?' 'Hadn't I found that?'

But indeed, although I have lived amongst agricultural labourers a good deal at one time or another, I would cheerfully acknowledge that his knowledge—at any rate of their psychologies—had a great deal more insight than my own. He had such an extraordinary gift for observing minutiae—and a gift still more extraordinary for making people talk. I have heard the secretary of a golf club, a dour silent man who never addressed five words to myself though I was one of his members, talk for twenty minutes to the Master about a new bunker that he was thinking of making at the fourteenth hole. And James had never touched a niblick in his life. It was the same with market-women, tram-conductors, ship-builders' labourers, auctioneers. I have stood by and heard them talk to him for hours. Indeed, I am fairly certain that he once had a murder confessed to him. But he needed to stand on extraordinarily firm ground before he would think that he knew a world. And what he knew he rendered, along with its amenities, its gentlefolkishness, its pettinesses, its make-believes. He gives you an immense—and an increasingly tragic picture of a Leisured Society that is fairly unavailing, materialist, emasculated—and doomed. No one was more aware of all that than he.

Steevie used to rail at English Literature, as being one immense petty, Parlour Game. Our books he used to say were written by men who never wanted to go out of drawing-rooms for people who wanted to live at perpetual tea-parties. Even our adventure stories, colonial fictions and tales of the boundless prairie were conducted in that spirit. The criticism was just enough. It was possible that James never wanted to live outside tea-parties—but the tea-parties that he wanted were debating circles of a splendid aloofness, of an immense human sympathy, and of a beauty that you do not find in Putney—or in Passy!

It was his tragedy that no such five o'clock ever sounded for him on the timepieces of this world. And that is no doubt the real tragedy of all of us—of all societies—that we never find in our Spanish Castle our ideal friends living in an assured and permanent republic. Crane's Utopia, but not his literary method, was different. He gave you the pattern in—and the reverse of—the carpet in physical life—in wars, in slums, in Western saloons, in a world where the 'gun' was the final argument. The life that Conrad gives you is somewhere halfway between the two: it is dominated—but less dominated—by the revolver than that of Stephen Crane, and dominated, but less dominated, by the moral scruple than that of James. But the approach to life is the same with all these three: they show you that disillusionment is to be found alike at the tea-table, in the slum and on the tented field. That is of great service to our Republic.

It occurs to me that I have given a picture of Henry James in which small personal unkindlinesses may appear to sound too dominant a note. That is the misfortune of wishing to point a particular moral. I will not say that loveableness was the predominating feature of the Old Man: he was too intent on his own particular aims to be lavishly sentimental over surrounding humanity. And his was not a character painted in the flat, in water-colour, like the caricatures of Rowlandson. For some protective reason or other, just as Shelley used to call himself the Atheist, he loved to appear in the character of a sort of Mr Pickwick—with the rather superficial benevolences, and the mannerisms of which he was perfectly aware. But below that protective mask was undoubtedly a plane of nervous cruelty. I have heard him be—to simple and quite unpretentious people—more diabolically blighting than it was quite decent for a man to be—for he was always an artist in expression. And it needed a certain fortitude when, the studied benevolence and the chuckling, savouring, enjoyment of words, disappearing suddenly from his personality, his dark eyes rolled in their whites and he spoke very brutal and direct English. He chose in fact to appear as Henrietta Maria—but he could be atrocious to those who behaved as if they took him at that valuation.

And there was yet a third depth—a depth of religious, of mystical benevolence such as you find just now and again in the stories that he 'wanted' to write—in *The Great Good Place*.... His practical benevolences were innumerable, astonishing—and indefatigable. To do a kindness when a sick cat or dog of the human race *had* 'got through' to his mind as needing assistance he would exhibit all the extraordinary ingenuities that are displayed in his most involved sentences.

I have said that my relation with James was in no sense literary—and I never knew what it *was*. I am perfectly sure that I never in my life addressed to the Master one word of praise or of flattery and, as far as I know, he called me *le jeune homme modeste* and left it at that. He did indeed confess to having drawn my externals in Merton Densher of *The Wings of the Dove*—the longish, leanish, loosish, rather vague Englishman who, never seeming to have anything to do with his days, occupied in journalism his night hours.

I daresay he took me to be a journalist of a gentle disposition, too languid to interrupt him. Once, after I had sent him one of my volumes of poems, he just mentioned the name of the book, raised both his hands over his head, let them slowly down again, made an extraordinary, quick grimace, and shook with an immense internal joke.... Shortly afterwards he began to poke fun at Swinburne.

In revenge, constantly and with every appearance of according weight to my opinions, though he seldom waited for an answer, he would consult me about practical matters —investments now and then, agreements once or twice— and, finally, unceasingly as to his fantastic domestic arrangements. He had at one stage portentous but increasingly unsatisfactory servants of whom, in his kindness of heart, he would not get rid until their conduct became the talk of the Antient Town of Rye.

So, one day he came over to Winchelsea to ask me if

I thought a Lady Help would be a desirable feature in an eminent bachelor's establishment.... Going as we seemed eternally in those days to be doing, down Winchelsea Hill under the Strand Gate, he said:

'H ... you seem worried!' I said that I was worried. I don't know how he knew. But he knew everything.

Ellen Terry waved her gracious hand from the old garden above the tower; the collar of Maximilian the dachshund called for adjustment. He began another interminable, refining, sentence—about housemaids and their locutions. It lasted us to the bridge at the western foot of Rye.

In Rye High Street he exclaimed—he was extraordinarily flustered:

'I perceive a compatriot. Let us go into this shop!' And he bolted into a fruiterer's. He came out holding an orange and, eventually, throwing it into the air in an ecstasy of nervousness and stuttering like a schoolboy:

'If it's money H ...' he brought out. *'Mon sac n'est pas grand ... Mais puisez dans mon sac!'*

I explained that it was not about money that I was worried, but about the 'form' of a book I was writing. His mute agony was a painful thing to see. He became much more appalled, but much less nervous. At last he made the great sacrifice:

'Well, then,' he said, 'I'm supposed to be.... Um, um.... There's Mary ... Mrs Ward ... does me the honour.... I'm supposed to know.... In short: Why not let me look at the manuscript!'

I had the decency not to take up his time with it.... *Les beaux jours quand on était bien modeste!* And how much I regret that I did not.

The last time I saw him was, accidentally, in August of 1915—on the fourteenth of that month, in St James's Park. He said:

'Tu vas te battre pour le sol sacré de Mme. de Stael!'

I suppose it was characteristic that he should say 'de Mme. de Stael'—and not of Stendhal, or even of George

69

Sand! He added—and how sincerely and with what passion—putting one hand on his chest and just bowing, that he loved and had loved France as he had never loved a woman!

I have said that I remember only one occasion on which Henry James spoke of his own work. That was like this: He had published *The Sacred Fount,* and was walking along beside the little shipyard at the foot of Rye Hill. Suddenly he said:

'You understand. . . . I *wanted* to write *The Great Good Place* and *The Altar of the Dead.* There are things one wants to write all one's life but one's artist's conscience prevents one. . . . And then . . . perhaps one allows oneself. . . .'

I don't know what he meant. . . . Or I do! For there *are* things one wants to write all one's life—only one's artist's conscience prevents one. That is the first—or the final, bitter—lesson that the Artist has to learn.

MR JAMES AND MR KIPLING

Lamb House was a majestic Georgian building of the type that Henry James had gone to England more especially to seek. Its best front gave on to the garden. The garden had an immense smooth lawn and was shut in by grey stone walls against which grew perennial flowers. It contained also a massively built white-panelled pavilion. In that, during the summer at least, the Master usually sat and worked.

In Rye church you could see the remains of a criminal hung in chains. It was that of a murderer, a butcher, who set out to kill a Mr Lamb and killed a Mr Greville. Or it may have been the other way round. Rye Town was prouder of its murderer than of its two literary lights, Fletcher and Henry James, but he always seemed to me to have been a clumsy fellow. Lamb House had belonged to the family of the gentleman who was—or wasn't—killed. But Henry James most gloated over the other legend according to which the house had been occupied by a mistress of George IV. The King, sailing down channel on a battleship, was said to have been rowed ashore to visit the lady in the garden pavilion. I always used to wonder at the prodigious number of caps, gloves, canes and hats that were arranged on a table—or it may have been a great chest—in the hall. How, I used to say to myself, can he need so prodigious a number of head-coverings? And I would wonder what thoughts revolved in his head whilst he selected the cap or the stick of the day. I never myself possessed more than one cloth cap at a time.

When I was admitted into his presence by the astonishingly ornate manservant he said:

'A writer who unites—if I may use the phrase—in his own person an enviable popularity to—as I am told—considerable literary gifts and whom I may say I like because he treats me'—and here Mr James laid his hand over his heart, made the slightest of bows and, rather cruelly rolling his dark and liquid eyes and moving his lower jaw as if he were rolling in his mouth a piquant tit-bit, Mr James continued, 'because he treats me—if again I may say any such thing—with proper respect'—and there would be an immense humorous gasp before the word 'respect'—...'I refer of course to Mr Kipling...has just been to see me. And—such are the rewards of an enviable popularity!—a popularity such as I—or indeed you my young friend if you have any ambitions which I sometimes doubt—could not dream of far less imagine to ourselves—such are the rewards of an enviable popularity that Mr Kipling is in the possession of a magnificent one thousand two hundred guinea motor car. And, in the course of conversation as to characteristics of motor cars in general and those of the particular one thousand two hundred guinea motor car in the possession of our

friend.... But what do I say? ... Of our cynosure! Mr
Kipling uttered words which have for himself no doubt
a particular significance but which to me at least convey
almost literally nothing beyond their immediate sound....
Mr Kipling said that the motor car was calculated to make
the Englishman ... '—and again came the humorous gasp
and the roll of the eyes—'was calculated to make the Eng-
lishman ... think.' And Mr James abandoned himself for
part of a second to low chuckling. 'And,' he continued,
'the conversation dissolved itself, after digressions on the
advantages attendant on the possession of such a vehicl-
into what I believe are styled golden dreams—such as
how the magnificent one thousand two hundred guinea
motor car after having this evening conveyed its master
and mistress to Batemans Burwash of which the proper
pronunciation is Burridge would to-morrow devotedly re-
turn here and reaching here at twelve would convey me
and my nephew Billiam to Burridge in time to lunch and
having partaken of that repast to return here in time to
give tea to my friend Lady Maud Warrender who is
honouring that humble meal with her presence to-morrow
under my roof.... And we were all indulging in—what
is it?—delightful anticipations and dilating on the agree-
ablenesses of rapid—but not for fear of the police and
consideration for one's personal safety *too* rapid—speed
over country roads and all, if I may use the expression,
was gas and gingerbread when.... There is a loud knock-
ing on the door and—*avec des yeux éffarés* ... ' and here
Mr James really did make his prominent and noticeable
eye almost stick out of his head ... ' in rushes the chauf-
feur.... And in short the chauffeur has omitted to lubri-
cate the wheels of the magnificent one thousand two hun-
dred guinea motor car with the result that its axles have
become one piece of molten metal.... The consequence
is that its master and mistress will return to Burwash
which should be pronounced Burridge by train, and the
magnificent one thousand two hundred guinea motor car
will *not* devotedly return here at noon and will *not* in

time for lunch convey me and my nephew Billiam to
Burwash and will *not* return here in time for me to give
tea to my friend Lady Maud Warrender who is honouring
that humble meal with her presence to-morrow beneath
my roof or if the whether is fine in the garden. . . .'

'Which,' concluded the Master after subdued 'ho, ho,
ho's' of merriment, 'is calculated to make Mr Kipling
think.'

COLLABORATING WITH CONRAD

I

I may as well dispose, once and for all, of the legend that
I had any part in teaching Conrad English, though on
the face of it it may well look plausible enough since he
was a foreigner who never till the end of his life spoke
English other than as a foreigner. But when it came to
writing, it was at once quite a different matter. As I said
elsewhere a little time ago, the moment he got a pen in
his hand and had no eye to publication, Conrad could
write English with a speed, a volubility, and a banal
correctness that used to amaze me. So you have his
immense volume of letters. On the other hand, when, as
it were, he was going before the public, a species of stage
fright would almost completely paralyse him so that his
constructions were frequently very un-English.

In his letters, that is to say, he just let himself go with-
out precision of phrase as without *arrière pensée,* pouring
out supplications, abuse of third parties, eternal and un-
varying complaints, so that in the end the impression is
left of a weak, rather whining personality. But no impres-
sion could be more false. Conrad was a man, a He-man
if you like, who fought against enormous odds with un-
dying—with almost unfaltering courage. And his courage
was all the more impressive in that by birth, race, and

temperament he was an unshakable pessimist. Life for him was predestined to end tragically, or, if not, in banality; literature was foredoomed to failure. These were his *choses données*, his only certain truths. In face of that creed, his struggles were unceasing.

And it was astonishing what small things could call down to his underlying buoyancy. I remember once we had been struggling with *Romance* for hours and hours, and he had been in complete despair, and everything that I had suggested had called forth his bitterest gibes, and he was sick, and over ears in debt, and penniless. And we had come to a blank full-stop—one of those intervals when the soul *must* pause to breathe and love itself have rest. And Mrs Conrad came in and said that the mare had trotted from Postling Vents to Sandling in five minutes—say, twelve miles an hour! At once, there in the room was Conrad-Jack-ashore! The world was splendid; hope nodded from every rosebud that looked over the window-sill of the low room. We were going to get a car and go to Canterbury; the mare should have a brand-new breeching strap. And in an incredibly short space of time—say, three hours—at least half a page of *Romance* got itself written.

That was how it went, day in day out, for years—the despair, the lamentations continuing for hours, and then the sudden desperate attack on the work—the attack that would become the fabulous engrossment. We would write for whole days, for half nights, for half the day, or all the night. We would jot down passages on scraps of paper or on the margins of books, handing them one to the other or exchanging them. We would roar with laughter over passages that would have struck no other soul as humorous; Conrad would howl with rage and I would almost sigh over others that no other soul perhaps would have found as bad as we considered them. We would recoil one from the other and go each to our own cottage—our cottages at that period never being further the one from the other than an old mare could take us in

74

an afternoon. In those cottages we would prepare other drafts and so drive backwards and forwards with packages of manuscript under the dog-cart seats. We drove in the heat of summer, through the deluges of autumn, with the winter snows blinding our eyes. But always, always with manuscripts. Heavens, don't my fingers still tingle with the feeling of undoing the stiff buckles, long past midnight, of a horse streaming with rain—and the rubbing down in the stable and the backing the cart into the coach-house. And with always at the back of the mind, the consideration of some unfinished passage, the puzzledom to avoid some too-used phrase that yet seemed hypnotically inevitable.

II

He used to come in in the mornings and, having climbed the many stairs to my small, dreadful study, would sit for hours motionless and numb with a completely expressionless face. Every now and then he would say:

'I can't do it. It can't be done. *Je suis foutu!*' Then he would launch out into a frightful diatribe against the English language. It was a language for dogs and horses. It was incapable of conveying human thoughts. He had given up the attempt. For good. The damn paper must go without its damn serial. Who would care? No one.

I would stand in the window, looking right over London: a grey expanse with sparkling points. From there—in the middle West—one could see Greenwich Observatory in the extreme East. It was looking over that view that I first told Conrad the story that he turned into *The Secret Agent*.

But in those moments I would have a perfectly vacant mind. It just stopped. There was really nothing to say. English is not a good language for prose. You cannot make a direct statement in literary English. At any rate in those days you could not and I doubt if you can now —in English English. In American English you almost can, but you shock elegant ears. Conrad's English however was literary. I had nothing with which to console him.

He would declare that he had written the last word of that serial. I would manoeuvre him towards writing as the drake manoeuvres the sitting duck back to the nest when she has abandoned her eggs. I would read over his last sentence to him. If it provoked no beginnings on his part I would displace him at the desk and write a sentence or two. There are five words that seem horrible to me. They are *The Silver of the Mine*. That was the title of the part of *Nostromo* over which we then travailed.

He would groan:

'No, it's no use. I'm going to France. I tell you I am going to set up as a French writer. French is a language: it is not a collection of grunted sounds.'

I would say:

'*Nostromo* would go admirably in French. Let us get it blocked out. Then you could re-write it very easily in French.'

The hospital nurse would come in:

'Now, Mr Ford, it is time you got back to bed again.' I would have been up an hour.

Conrad liked the society of that nurse. Inscrutably. She was a flail. She had a face like a Cockney camel. Words that I hardly understood poured out of it incessantly. Conrad however did understand her. He had served before the mast with Cockney deckhands. He would ask her how her other patients were. That would give her an excuse to get going.

'Last peetien I ad wus Lord Northcliffe. Hoperishun on is leg! Lie in bed e would wiv the telephone on is chess. Sweer into the telephone e would. Sweer ... somethin' awful.... Sweer wen hi chinged im ... oh terrible. Sweer at the pines an then onto the telephone. At the *Dily Mile*. Sech lengwidge. Houtrageous. Then wen hi was going: "Nurse," e sez to me, "Nurse.... Whenever you hear men speak against me you will say: 'He bore his illness like a Christian and a gentleman.' " ... Peetient bifor that was an old maid ... bifor er they ad swingin doors. Between the quality staircase and the servants'. ... Green bize. ...' She had been standing on the top landing of the house. A servant let the green baize door swing against her. It had precipitated her down several flights of stone stairs. She lay at the bottom with her skull smashed and her brains protruding. The servants put sheets of newspaper under her head. They wanted to protect their mistress's staircase. When the surgeon came he could read the imprint of the paper on her brain— an account of the dispersal of the works of art from the collection of the Hon. Matthew L. Oldroyd.

That was her story—one of hundreds. Of thousands, perhaps. Her appearance used to drive me frantic. It meant that Conrad would not get to work for hours. Neither could I. I need a certain period of quiet and collection before words will come.

I would slip away downstairs and dust the dining-room against lunch. When I returned Conrad would be writing contentedly at my desk. The nurse with her lack-lustre eyes and untidy strands of hair hanging from beneath her cap was detrimental to all her patients. Conrad she seemed to stimulate. He would listen to her singular tarra-diddles for hours with an expression of the utmost interest and deference. Perhaps *Nostromo* would never have got itself written but for her. Or perhaps Conrad's next book would have borne a Parisian imprint.

W. H. HUDSON

Hudson was born of American parentage in a place called Quilmes in the Argentine, about 1840, and coming to London in the 'eighties of the last century, he was accustomed to declare—in order to account for his almost impassioned love for the English countryside—that no member of his family had been in England for over two hundred and fifty years. After his death his industrious and devoted biographer, Mr Morley Roberts, ferreted out that Hudson's father had been born in the State of Maine about 1814, his paternal grandfather having gone there from the West of England a little before the Declaration of Independence. On his mother's side he was, however, of very old United States descent. In any case his youth and young manhood had been passed in Spanish-American countries and that no doubt gave him his gravity of behaviour . . . and of prose. For he remained always an extraordinarily closed-up person and the legends that grew up about him could hardly be distinguished from the little biographical truths that one knew. The truths always came in asides. You would be talking about pumas. For this beast he had a great affection, calling it the friend of man. He would declare that the puma would follow a traveller for days over the pampas or through the forest, watch over him and his horse whilst he slept, and drive away the jaguar . . . who was the enemy of man. He said that this had happened to him many times. Once he had been riding for two months on the pampas, sleeping beneath the *ombu* trees that seem to cover half a county, and three times a puma had driven off a jaguar. It had been a period of drought. For a whole week he had not been able to wash his face. One asked what it was like not to wash one's face for a week and he would reply: 'Disagreeable. . . . Not so bad . . . as if cobwebs touched you here and there.' You would say that that must have been a disagreeable week all the same and he would slip out: 'Not so bad as a week I've known . . . when Mrs Hudson and I passed a whole ten days in a garret with nothing but a couple of tins of cocoa and some oatmeal to eat. . . .'

He shared with Turgenev the quality that makes you unable to find out how he got his effects. Like Turgenev he was utterly undramatic in his methods, and his books have that same quality that have those of the author of *Fathers and Children*. When you read them you forget the lines and the print. It is as if a remotely smiling face looked up at you out of the page and told you things. And those things become part of your own experience. It is years and years since I first read *Nature in Downland*. Yet, as I have already said somewhere or other, the first words that I there read have become a part of my own life. They describe how, lying on the turf of the high sunlit downs above Lewes in Sussex, Hudson looked up into the perfect, limpid blue of the sky and saw, going to infinite distances one behind the other, the eye picking up one, then another beyond it, and another and another, until the whole sky was postulated . . . little shining globes, like soap bubbles. They were thistledown floating in an almost windless heaven.

Now that is part of my life. I have never had the patience—the contemplative tranquillity—to lie looking up into the heavens. I have never in my life done it. Yet that is I, not Hudson, looking up into the heavens, the eye discovering more and more tiny, shining globes until the whole sky is filled with them, and those thistle-seed globes seem to be my globes.

For that is the quality of great art—and its use. It is you, not another, who at night with the stars shining have leaned over a Venice balcony and talked about patines of bright gold; you, not anyone else, saw the parents of Bazarov realize that their wonderful son was dead. And you yourself heard the voice cry, *Eli, Eli, lama sabacthani*! . . . because of the quality of the art with which those scenes were projected. . . .

His wife then—and it was at least true that in her day she had been a celebrated singer—kept a boardinghouse. She was twenty years older than Hudson and did not come up to his elbow. And it was more or less true that after her marriage to him she sang very little, because her voice was leaving her. But otherwise she was very normal and quick-witted, if a little quick-tempered and not a good business woman. For all the great money she had earned in her day had gone and shortly after their

10*

marriage her boarding-house went bankrupt too. It was then that they had known days of real starvation and it is not the least romantic part of Hudson's career, the desperate and courageous efforts he made to keep them going. He was a stranger in London with nothing to earn a living by but his pen; and it is curious to think that one of the ways by which he did earn money was by ferreting out genealogical tables for Americans of English origins. Then he also did hack-work descriptions of South American birds for scientific ornithologists who had never seen a bird. And then magazines began to commission him for articles about birds; his wife inherited a fantastically gloomy house in the most sooty neighbourhood of London and a small sum of money with which she set up a boarding-house that this time did not fail. And it was touching to see how Hudson made another gentle legend for himself amongst Shetland-shawled old maids and broken-down Indian colonels. And then he was granted a pension on the King's Civil List, and then fame came to him in London and money from New York. And he and his wife lived together until she died, a little before him, at the great age of a hundred years. . . . That, too, was Romance.

I am ashamed to say that I did not see it at the time, and I disliked the atmosphere of the boarding-house so much that whenever I could I used to insist on Hudson's coming out with me to Kensington Gardens. He was not a good walker in those days in spite of the fact that he had spent the greater part of his life on his feet, watching birds. We used to pace very slowly up and down beneath the tall elms of the Broad Walk and in front of the little palace, amongst the children of the wealthy. We would watch the grey squirrels that had come from New York and that were monstrously at home in the Gardens, having bitten off the tails of all the aboriginal red squirrels. And he would talk of how the Liberator carried his whip and reviewed his troops; and of the birds and herds and great trees of the pampas, far away and long ago. And *Far Away and Long Ago* is the most self-revelatory of all his books.

I do not think that I would much like to recapture many of the atmospheres of my own past. The present days are better. But I would be glad, indeed, if once again I could walk slowly along the dingy streets that led from that Bayswater boarding-house to Paddington Station ... slowly beside Hudson and his wife who would be going away towards English greennesses, through the most lugubrious streets the world could imagine, let alone know. And Huddie would be expressing theories as to the English rain and far below him his tiny wife would be incessantly telling him that he was going the wrong way.

Hudson had lived in that district for forty years, continuing to stay there after fortune had a little smiled on him—because it was near the great terminus of Paddington and they could slip away from there to the country without attracting attention by their singular disproportion in size. In spite of this they never could go to that exit from London without her telling him that he was going the wrong way ... I suppose because she had lived there for nearly a century. And she would keep on and on at it, bickering like a tiny wren threatening some great beast approaching her nest in the gorse. Her great age only affected her coloration so that she seemed to recede further and further into the mists of St Luke's Road until she was almost invisible. But her vivacity was unconquerable, and appropriate. It was as if, having framed that romantic giant, the force of nature could go no further, and to frame a fitting mate must compound for him that singular and elfish humming-bird.

A KIND OF CRITICISM

It is goodwill that is needed if the Humaner Letters are to come into their own. No amount of praise from Academicians will make a bad book have a permanent life whilst ill-natured comment on a good one will delay its entry into its kingdom. Thus people die without having read it and the writer is discouraged. These are the two worst things that can happen to humanity. You may die reconciled to your fate without having seen Carcassonne but what would it be like to leave the world without having read ... oh, *The Playboy of the Western World*? And what is the place in the hereafter reserved for the gentleman who checked the activities of Keats? For myself I would rather see the worst popular writer roll in gold than a fraudulent pill maker or a Wall Street bear. He at least is only doing what Shakespeare tried to do.

The only human activity that has always been of extreme importance to the world is imaginative literature. It is of supreme importance because it is the only means by which humanity can express at once emotions and ideas. To avoid controversy I am perfectly ready to concede that the other arts are of equal importance. But nothing that is not an art is of any lasting importance at all, the meanest novel being humanly more valuable than the most pompous of factual works, the most formidable of material achievements or the most carefully thought out of legal codes. Samuel Butler wrote an immense number of wasted words in the attempt to avenge himself for some fancied slight at the hands of Darwin. But, in spite of these follies, *The Way of All Flesh* is of vastly more use to us to-day than is *The Origin of Species*. Darwin as scientist is as superseded as the poor alchemist in the Spessart inn: so is Butler in the same department of human futility. But *The Way of All Flesh* cannot be superseded because it is a record of humanity. Science changes its aspect as every new investigator gains sufficient publicity to discredit his predecessors. The stuff of humanity is unchangeable. I do not expect the lay reader to agree with me in this pronouncement but it would be better for him if he did. The world would be a clearer place to him.

From that point of view the activities of the old *Athenaeum* under Maccoll were unmitigatedly harmful—

82

and singularly adroit. Mr Maccoll was to all appearances, a nearly imbecile, blond, bald, whiskered individual. He wore black gloves on every occasion indoors or out, and if you addressed him his eyes wandered round the cornice of the ceiling as if the mere fact of being spoken to had driven him into a panic. As far as I know he never wrote anything except perhaps the biography of some obscure theologian or diplomatist but his bulky figure with its black kid gloves—and its hand in addition always in the pockets of his reefer jacket as if he had doubly to hide some grotesque and shameful disease—his panic-stricken and bulky figure comes back to me as containing one of the most potent and disastrous forces of his day.

He had got his job, I think, from having been the travelling tutor of Sir Charles Dilke, the politician and owner of the journal. But having made his singular and bemused apparition at a public or private function he would return to his office and with unerring and diabolical skill would send out books to the reviewers for whom they were exactly unsuited. The policy of his journal was to regard all novels as tawdry trifles to be dismissed in a few notes. It considered that no poetry had been written or could have been written by persons born after 1820, except when Mr Watts-Dunton got hold of a volume by D. G. Rossetti whose solicitor he was or by Swinburne to whom he acted as keeper. The body of the paper was given up to tremendous and sesquipedalian reviews of works with titles like: *The Walcheren Expedition and the Manoeuvres in the Low Countries* in three volumes, post quarto. If its reviewer could discover three misprints, the name of a Dutch village spelt wrong, two real inaccuracies, and a nine which the printer had inverted in a date so that it looked like a six—then the joy of the journal was unmeasured. It pronounced in Olympian tones that this immense undertaking was completely worthless to the student of the subject and nothing could better display its infallibility. It once received a novel of mine with the words:

'From the fact that on page 276 Mr Hueffer misspells the word *herasia* the reader will be able to judge of the value of his piece of fiction,' and most novels received as summary treatment at its hands.

THE APOTHEOSIS OF JOHN GALSWORTHY

He made towards supreme honours a tranquil course that suggested that of a white-sailed ship progressing inevitably across a halcyon sea. You would have said that he had every blessing that kings and peoples and Providence had to bestow. Having refused a knighthood he was awarded the highest honour that the King had at his disposal—that of the Order of Merit. He presided in Paris at the dinner of the international P.E.N. Club, which is the highest honour that the members of his craft could find for him; and, in the end, the Nobel Prize Committee honoured itself by selecting him for one of its laureates. It seemed, all this, appropriate and inevitable, for, in honouring him, the world honoured one of its noblest philanthropists.

The last time I saw him was in Paris when he gave his presidential address to his beloved P.E.N. And singularly, as he emerged above the shadow of all those hard French writers, there re-emerged at any rate for me the sense of his frailty . . . of his being something that must be shielded from the harder earnestnesses of the world. I don't know that he was conscious on that last public triumph of the really bad nature of the hard men who surrounded him. The world had moved onward since the days when he had read Maupassant and Turgenev for what he could learn of them. Both those writers were what he called dissolvents and the Paris *littérateurs* now wanted above all constructive writing and would have agreed with him if he had said— as he did in one of the last letters that he wrote—that Tolstoi was a greater writer than Turgenev.

But, there, he said nothing of the sort. He seemed to float, above all those potential assassins, like a white swan above a gloomy mere, radiating bright sunlight... and with his gentle, modest French words he made statements that ran hissing through Paris as if he had drawn a whip across all those listening faces.

For the French writer of to-day, Maupassant is the Nihilist Enemy—an enemy almost as hated as the late M. Anatole France.

And Turgenev is an alien ugly duckling who once disgusted the paving-stones of Paris with his foreign footsteps. Nothing indeed so infuriates the French of to-day as to say that Turgenev was really a French writer.... And there, enthroned and smiling, poor Galsworthy told that audience that shivered like tigers in a circus cage that, if he had trained himself to have any art, and if that training had landed him where he was, that art had been that of French writers.

A sort of buzzing of pleasurable anticipation went all round that ferocious assembly. The author of *Fort Comme La Paix* looked at the author of *Nuits Ensoleillées* and thought: 'Aha, my friend, this is going to be a bitter moment for you. When I consider the *dédicace* of the ignoble volume that this barbarian chieftain presented yesterday to me... when I consider the fulsome, but nevertheless deserved, praise that he wrote on that fly-leaf, I don't have to doubt whom he is going to claim as his Master....' And the author of *Nuits Ensoleillées* looked back at the author of the other classic and thought exactly the same thing—with the necessary change in the identity of the author. And every French author present looked at every other French author and thought thoughts similar. And when the applause subsided poor Jack went on:

Yes, he repeated, all the art he had had he had had of the French. If he stood where he was, if he was honoured as he was, it was because all his long life he had studied the works, he had been guided by the examples of... Guy de Maupassant and of him who though a foreigner by

birth was yet more French in heart than any Frenchman—
Ivan Turgenev!

I have never seen an audience so confounded. If an
invisible force had snatched large, juicy joints of meat from
the very jaws of a hundred Bengal tigers the effect would
have been the same. They simply could not believe their
ears. . . . As for me, I was so overwhelmed with confusion
that I ran out of that place and plunged, my cheeks still
crimson, into the salon of the author of *Vasco*, who was
preparing to give a tea-party at the end of the Île St Louis.
And the news had got there before me. It was in the salon
of every author of the Île, of the Rue Guynemer, of the
Rues Madame, Jacob, Tombe Issoire, and Notre-Dame des
Champs, before the triumphant Galsworthy had finished
his next sentence. . . . For that was the real triumph of his
radiant personality, that not one of the fierce beasts quiver-
ing under his lash so much as raised a protest. No other
man in the world could have brought that off!

PORTRAIT OF THE ARTIST AS A DANDY

YOU are to think of me then as rather a dandy. I was going through that phase. It lasted perhaps eight years—until Armageddon made one dress otherwise. Every morning about eleven you would see me issue from the door of my apartment. I should be wearing a very long morning coat, a perfectly immaculate high hat, lavender trousers, a near-Gladstone collar, and a black satin stock. As often as not, at one period, I should be followed by a Great Dane. The dog actually belonged to Stephen Reynolds but he disliked exercising it in London because he was nervous at crossings. But a policeman will always stop the traffic for a Great Dane to cross. I carried a malacca cane with a gold knob.

I would walk up Holland Park Avenue as far as the entrance to Kensington Gardens, diagonally across them to Rotten Row where I would cross to St James's Park and the Green Park, cross them and reach one or other of my clubs about half-past twelve, read the papers and my letters until one. Then I would lunch at the club or the Carlton and take a hansom—later a taxi—back to my apartment which I would reach about half-past two. At five I would go to or give a tea-party. Before dinner I would take a bath and a barber would come in and shave me. I dined out every day, but very occasionally, for someone special I would cook a dinner myself in my own flat, putting a chef's coat over my evening things. I had two boasts, the one that no one had ever seen me work, the other that I walked four miles every day on grass. That was in crossing

87

the parks. In Central Park, New York, I had been apostrophized by a policeman who said:

'Get off the grass, same as you would in any other civilized country.' I used my second boast usually on New Yorkers, of whom I saw a good many.

My father used to say that he was the laziest man in the world, yet he had done more work than any man living. I could almost say as much of myself. I fancy that for ten years—say from 1904 to 1914—I never took a complete day's rest. I worked even on the trains in America at a time when that was less usual than it is to-day. My record in the British Museum Catalogue fills me with shame; it occupies page on page with the mere titles of my printed work. Even at that it is not a complete record; it omits several books published only in America. I do not imagine that anyone not a daily journalist has written as much as I have and I imagine that few daily journalists have written more.

I do not say that I am proud of the record. If I had written less I should no doubt have written better. Of the fifty-two odd separate books there catalogued probably forty are out of print. There is only one of those forty that I should care to re-publish and of the remaining twelve there are not more than six of which I should much regret the disappearance.

This great body of work was produced without any feeling of fatigue. At the time of which I am writing I used to work with great regularity from nine to eleven when I went out to lunch and from half-past two to half-past four when I would go out to tea. After I was eighteen I never wrote at night and except for a week or so before the publication of the first number of the *English Review* I never did any work at all—even editing or proof correcting—after dinner. In the four hours of work I turned out exactly 2,000 words. Of these I would condemn about half. This left about 1,000 words for the day. A thousand words a day is 365,000 for the year—enough to make over four novels. Of course I never published four novels in any one year. Only twice indeed have I published as many as two. The usual tale was one novel and one book of the type called in England 'serious.' There the novel can never be heralded as 'serious.' It would give the public cause to think the writer was in earnest which to the Englishman is insupportable. In the United States books that are not novels are classed as 'non-fiction.' The classification is perhaps not accurate but it is more complimentary to the novelist. That I suppose is why I have latterly published more books to the west than to the east of the Atlantic. Earnestness *will* come creeping into what I write.

A LITERARY PARTY

The year was 1903. Those digits added up to thirteen. No one should have done anything in that year. Or it was perhaps because the house I then took was accursed. It was a monstrous sepulchre—and not even whitened. It was grey with the greyness of withered bones. It was triangular in ground plan: the face formed the nose of a blunted redan, the body tapered to a wedge in which there was a staircase like the corkscrew staircases of the Middle Ages. The façade was thus monstrous, the tail ignoble. It was seven stories in height and in those days elevators in private houses were unknown. It was what housemaids call: 'A Murderer.'

The happenings in that house come back to me as gruesome and bizarre. I daresay they were merely normal. They were mere episodes in the chain of disasters, suicides, bankruptcies, and despairs that visited its successive tenants and owners. My first party was distinguished by Conrad's attack on the unfortunate Mr Charles Lewis Hind. This violent encounter took place in a circle of half-gay, half-morose celebrities. Mr James had brought Mrs Humphry Ward; Mrs Clifford, who could be as awful as Mrs Ward, had brought some mild and decorous young American—I should think it was Mr Owen Wister. Mr Watts-Dunton had brought a message from Swinburne, blessing me because he had known me as a baby. This he repeated *à tort et à travers* at the oddest and most inconvenient moments. He was deaf and accustomed to speaking to Swinburne who was deafer. I found myself distracted at odd moments by his rather snuffling, elevated voice exclaiming:

'Swinburne said in excusing himself for not attending this party of our gifted young host. . . .'

He was a little dark man with an immense waterfall of grey moustache. Finally he settled himself on, I think, the always patient Mr Galsworthy and repeated over and over again the message with which he was charged. Then I was aware that Conrad had hold of Lewis Hind's tie and was dragging him towards the door that gave on to the corkscrew staircase. If he had thrown Hind down it the poor man would have been killed. I managed to separate them but I haven't forgotten and don't suppose I ever shall forget the look of polite incredulity of the more august guests. Mrs Humphry Ward looked like a disgusted sheep. Mrs Clifford, who loved the society of reviewers, was openly distressed at the disappearance of Mr Hind. Mr Hind was the editor of the *Academy*. The *Academy* was a rather livelier *Athenaeum*. A great lady of the Court of His Majesty put her lorgnettes up to her proud nose and weary eyes and exclaimed to me afterwards:

'Haw! Very interesting. But awkward for you . . . I suppose all literary parties are like that.'

She added:

'I wonder you give 'em. I shouldn't. I once gave one but it did not work. Yet one tries to encourage . . . ah . . . these things!'

The court in those days had to be interested in Literature because Edward VII wanted to be told about books. I know this because I had at that date a secretary who was very highly connected. Her name was Smith and she was the daughter of a very famous soldier. She was one day sitting with the beautiful Lady Londonderry who was her cousin. Lady Londonderry was dying of a painful disease, but lay on a sofa. The King came in. Miss Smith was the shyest human being I have ever known. She desired to sink into the ground and made for the door. Lady Londonderry told her to stay and pour tea for them. Lady Londonderry presented her as 'Miss Smith, the daughter of the famous soldier.' The King said:

'Smith . . . ah we all know *that* name.' Royal politenesses must exact a certain lack of the sense of humour. . . .

Well; the King asked Lady Londonderry if he might touch the bell and ask the footman for some very dry toast as he was banting. Miss Smith poured tea. As she was finally escaping the King said:

'Miss Smith. Lady Londonderry tells me you are interested in literature. I like books. I like boys' books . . . Captain Marryat now. I have read all Captain Marryat. But I find it very difficult to get books like that.' He said that he had asked all the Court but no one could tell him of books like that. He added:

'If in the course of your researches at the British Museum, Miss Smith, you should come across any such books, I should be very much obliged if you would jot their names down on a postcard and send it to me, at Buckingham Palace.'

Miss Smith said it seemed to her curious that he should think she did not know his address.

STARTING A REVIEW

There entered then into me the itch of trying to meddle in English literary affairs. The old literary gang of the *Athenaeum-Spectator-Heavy Artillery* order was slowly decaying. Younger lions were not only roaring but making carnage of their predecessors. Mr Wells was then growing a formidable mane, Arnold Bennett if not widely known was at least known to and admired by me. Mr Wells had given me Bennett's first novel—*A Man From The North*. Experimenting in forms kept Conrad still young. Henry James was still 'young James' for my uncle William Rossetti and hardly known of by the general public. George Meredith and Thomas Hardy had come into their own only very little before, Mr George Moore was being forgotten as he was always being forgotten, Mr Yeats was known as having written the *Isle of Innisfree*. It seemed to me that if that nucleus of writers could be got together with what undiscovered talent the country might hold a Movement might be started. I had one or two things I wanted to say. They were about the technical side of novel writing. But mostly I desired to give the writers of whom I have spoken as it were a rostrum. It was with that idea that I had returned from America. England, I knew, would always regard me as, rather comically and a little suspiciously—too damn in earnest. The others it might listen to and I might slip a word in now and then.

The nature of the periodical to be started gave me a good deal of thought. To imagine that a magazine devoted to imaginative literature and technical criticism alone would find more than a hundred readers in the United Kingdom was a delusion that I in no way had. It must therefore of necessity be a hybrid, giving at least half its space to current affairs. Those I did not consider myself fit to deal with. I knew either nothing about them or I knew so much that I could not form any opinions. The only public matter as to which I was determined to take a line was that of female suffrage.

I dallied with the idea for some time. Then I came across the politician who had insisted on telling me his life history. I do not remember if he approached me or I him. At any rate we quickly came to an agreement. He was a virulent Tory of the new school and he wanted an organ of his own. He was to provide half of the capital necessary which we agreed was to be £5,000, I the other half. He was to edit half the magazine, which was to be a monthly, I the other half. Being a businessman as well as a politician he was to manage the business affairs of the concern, I to see to its make up, proof-reading, and other details of publication. It was a good arrangement. I liked him very much. He was too brilliant to like me extremely but he tolerated me more than he tolerated most people. He had an exaggerated idea of my omniscience and political influence.

I had arranged with the house of Duckworth to publish the *Review* and had commissioned a number of stories, poems, and critical articles. He came to me one day and said he could not supervise the business affairs of the concern. That was rather a heavy blow because I knew enough about business to know that I should make a muddle of that side of it. I sighed, cabled to Byles who was then in Japan to come back and take on the business of the *Review*, and consented to continue to enterprise. A little later my friend came to me and said that he could not undertake to do half the editing. A General Election was in the offing; he had neglected his constituency; he would have to go perpetually into the North to kick off footballs, open flower shows, subscribe to fox-hounds, and utter verbal coruscations. He suggested that I might find some one else of his school of thought to direct the political policy of the *Review*; I sighed again and consented. For that Marwood was indicated. He was an Old, rather than a New Tory and he was incurably indolent. But he consented to suggest from Winchelsea the sort of article that should go into the *Review* and in most cases to indicate the writers who should be invited to contribute. My political friend proposed in fairness that if so much of the labour was to fall on me he should increase the amount of capital that he found whilst I should retain my full half share of the control of the periodical. I was glad of that because I had lately had rather serious financial reverses.

The dummy of the first number approached completion; I had announced the name of the periodical, *The English Review*, in the press. It was Conrad who chose the title.

He felt a certain sardonic pleasure in the choosing so national a name for a periodical that promised to be singularly international in tone, that was started mainly in his not very English interest and conducted by myself who was growing every day more and more alien to the normal English trend of thought, at any rate in matters of literary technique. And it was matters of literary technique that almost exclusively interested both him and myself. That was very un-English.

A couple of presumably needy journalists, both of very great ability, conceived the idea of making me who was presumed to be rolling in wealth, pay for the use of that title. They registered it as soon as I had announced it in the press and then asked me to pay a prodigious sum for its use. I offered them half a sovereign a piece. They then published a single-sheet broad-sheet under the title of *The English Review.* Its letterpress consisted of virulent attacks on Lord Northcliffe and myself, promising extraordinary revelations as to both of us in their next number. I fancy they imagined that Lord Northcliffe was financing the review. The main allegation against myself was that I was a 'multiple reviewer.' The charge was true enough but only as far as one book was concerned. That was Charles Doughty's *Dawn in Britain*—an epic poem in twelve books and four volumes. I had a great admiration for Doughty, who was the author also of *Arabia Deserta* and I read his poem entirely through with a great deal of pleasure. No reviewer in London had leisure for that task. The book looked as if it might go unreviewed, so I asked a number of those gentlemen to let me review it for them. Others, hearing that I had volunteered to do it, also asked me to relieve them of the task. I do not remember how many reviews I wrote: it was a considerable number and some of them were quite long. I pleased myself by finding that I could do them all without once repeating a sentence or even an idea. At any rate I was quite unrepentant. I do not see why you should not write more than one review of a book for which you have a great admiration. I have written several times about *Ulysses*.

I continued to take no notice of the other *English Review*. My telephone became a constant worry because those two gentlemen rang me up at all hours of the night asking me to buy the title for sums that gradually descended from a thousand pounds to five. Lord Northcliffe on the other hand applied for an injunction against my rivals in one of the courts—I forget which. The injunction was granted and the other *English Review* disappeared. The real joke was that I had lent one of those lively persons the money with which he paid for his broadsheet. At any rate, just before he printed it, I had met him looking very destitute in Fleet Street and had lent him exactly the sum with which he paid his printer's and papermaker's bill.

A little later I went to a Trench dinner. A Trench dinner was a Dutch treat presided over by Herbert Trench, the Irish poet. They were agreeable affairs and attended by most of the brilliant people in London. I was only asked to one. On this occasion I was set at a round table with Mr Hilaire Belloc, Mr Gilbert Chesterton, Mr Maurice Baring, and Mr H. G. Wells. My politician was at another table with Mr Trench, the Marchioness of Londonderry and other notables.

Amongst all these celebrities I felt nervous. Celebrities are always rude to me. That has been the case from my tenderest years. I can hardly think of one that has not, at one time or another, said rude things to me. I ought to except politicians. I can hardly remember a politician who has not said nice things to me about my books—as soon as he heard that I was a writer. I suppose they learn that when canvassing for votes. Mr Balfour once asked me to send him my books as they came out. I did for years. He always wrote politely thanking me for the volume 'from the reading of which he anticipated much pleasure.' The letters were always marked: 'Not for publication.'

I knew I should not get through that dinner without

discomfort. It came. Mr Belloc was late. I had written
an article about him a day or two before. It had been
published that morning. I had classed him among the
brilliant *jeunes* of the day and had expressed the really
great admiration I felt for his wit, sincerity, and learning.
He hurried in, saw me, stopped as if he had been shot,
thrust his hand through his forelock, gave one more
maledictory glance at me with his baleful, pebble-blue
eyes and then sank wearily into his chair next to Mr
Maurice Baring. He looked anywhere but at me and began
an impassioned monologue about the misfortunes of
historians. They wore themselves out searching for matter
in the British Museum Library and other stuffy places;
they toiled till far into the night putting the results of
their researches on paper. After infinite tribulation they
published their books. Then along came the cold-eyed
critic.

I forget what Mr Belloc said that the cold-eyed critic
did to the historian but I realized that it was my eyes
that were frigid in his. In my eulogy of him I had amiably
found fault with some gigantic exaggeration in, I think,
a book about the Cromwell family. What exactly Thomas
Cromwell had done to our co-religionists or how Oliver
had sinned against the Church of Rome I forget. Heaven
forbid that I should set myself down as good a Papist
as Mr Belloc, but I dislike to think of myself as a worse.
I consider that there are only two human organizations
that are nearly perfect for their disparate functions. They
are the Church of Rome and His Britannic Majesty's
Army. I would cheerfully offer my life for either if it
would do them any good and supposing them not to be
arrayed the one against the other. But I could not see
that the cause of the Church was advantaged by gigantic-
ally exaggerating the confiscations from which she has
suffered any more than it would help the Old Contempti-
bles to represent them as having been without exception
teachers in Sunday Schools. I had said this mildly in my

article. As a matter of fact I wished that Mr Belloc would write novels and leave propaganda to the less gifted.

The affair ended dramatically in nothing, for before ending his monologue Mr Belloc suddenly burst out to some one whom I could not see at the chairman's table beside us:

'Our Lord! What do you know about Our Lord? Our Lord was a gentleman.'

After that I escaped notice in the shadow of Mr Chesterton. Mr Chesterton and Mr Belloc were one on each side of Mr Baring. They occupied themselves for some time in trying in vain to balance glasses of Rhine Wine on the skull of Mr Baring. That gentleman comes back to me as having been then only a little less bald than an egg. The floor and his shirt front received the wine in equal quantities. . . .

Suddenly Mr Belloc was at me again. He said that I would not dare to print in my *Review* any article that he sent me just as it stood. I said I would. He repeated that I would not and I that I would. He was in those days almost as vigorous a muck-raker as S. S. McClure and hardly anyone had the courage to print him in his more coruscating moments. I may say that I did print his article but, since it contained the most amazing accusations against bishops, keepers of the Crown jewels, West Indian Governors and other apparently unoffending and unimportant beings, I made the printer black out the names and functions of everybody concerned. Those pages of the *Review* startlingly resembled newspapers in Russia after they had received the attention of the censor. They startled Mr St Loe Strachey, the Editor of the *Spectator*, to some purpose. He confused my *English Review* with the broad-sheet promoted by the two journalists and supposed that either I or Mr Belloc intended to threaten the owners of the blacked out names with exposure in another number if we were not bought off. Solemnly and weightily he protested against this growing tendency in British journals. He seemed to me to be a mild and doting old gentleman, so I wrote to him amiably and told him that he had accused me of being a blackmailer and would he kindly refute himself in the next number of his journal. He did so and wrote me a very agitated letter, saying that he had meant nothing of the sort. He did not say what he *had* meant.

That Trench dinner, different as it was from the Trench dinners that we afterwards ate, came also to an end. I was going towards the Piccadilly Tube. It was pouring and Mr Belloc was begging me not to believe that he was in fact the light hearted being that he appeared. Actually he was filled with the woes of all the world.

I was beginning to assure him that from then on I would regard his as a figure of the deepest tragedy. We were just turning into the Tube Station when my politician, ex-fellow editor and business manager came running up rather breathlessly and caught hold of the arm of mine that Mr Belloc was not imprisoning. He said:

'Fordie, I'm very sorry. I can't find my half share of the capital for the *Review*.'

I said:

'That will be all right.' He disappeared and I went on assuring Mr Belloc of my appreciation of his pessimism.

It appeared subsequently that my friend was suffering from the same financial disaster that had hit hard not only myself but many other people. It was the case of a disappearance abroad with an expensive young woman of a man the bearer of a very honoured name in whose faith too many had reposed their trust. He subsequently committed suicide.

There seemed to be nothing to do but to close down that periodical, pay off the contributors whom I had already commissioned and realize my dream of retiring to a little farm in Provence. I had of course to tell Marwood who was by that time as enthusiastic about the *Review* as he could be about anything.

He agreed with me. There was nothing to do but to shut it down. He made a good many caustic remarks about Young Tories in general and my friend in particular. I disagreed with him. That politician was no more guilty than I. Marwood, however, was certain that he had never intended to find the money.

I returned from Winchelsea to Aldington where I had by now bought a cottage. There remained, it seemed, nothing for it but to emigrate to Provence and there seemed to be nowhere else to emigrate to. As the world then appeared to me I could support living in London if I had the *Review*. Without it, I couldn't.

I was writing to a friend I had in Tarascon—a *notaire* —to ask about small farms that might be for sale in his neighbourhood. It was a Sunday. Marwood was suddenly on the terrace. He was pale with indignation and brandished a crumpled newspaper. He panted:

'You've got to carry on that *Review*.'

I had never seen him agitated before—and I never did again. He must have got up at four that morning to catch the train from Winchelsea to Aldington.

The newspaper announced that the *Cornhill Magazine* had refused to print, on the score of immorality, a poem of Thomas Hardy called *A Sunday Morning Tragedy*. All the other heavy and semi-heavy monthlies, all the weeklies, all the daily papers in England had similarly refused. Marwood said:

'You must print it. We can't have the country made a laughing stock.' He was of opinion that the rest of the world must guffaw if it heard that Hardy could not find a publisher in England. Marwood was accustomed to say that nothing worth the attention of a grown man had been written in England since the eighteenth century. Clarendon's *History of the Great Rebellion* and the Jacobean poets were his reading. He made a great concession to modernity when he read Maine's *Ancient Law* and Doughty's *Arabia Deserta*. Yet there he was mad to spend several thousand pounds in order to publish one poem by a modern poet who as poet was hardly known at all. For, of course, he found the money that hadn't been found by my other friend.

That was *my* Sunday morning tragedy. But for that I should have been saved a great deal of labour, a number of enemies. I should have been, now, twenty years instead of only six months, a kitchen-gardener in Provence.

ENTER EZRA POUND

When I first knew him his Philadelphian accent was comprehensible if disconcerting; his beard and flowing locks were auburn and luxuriant; he was astonishingly meagre and agile. He threw himself alarmingly into frail chairs, devoured enormous quantities of your pastry, fixed his pince-nez firmly on his nose, drew out a manuscript from his pocket, threw his head back, closed his eyes to the point of invisibility and looking down his nose would chuckle like Mephistopheles and read you a translation from Arnaut Daniel. The only part of that *aubade* that you would understand would be the refrain:

'*Ah me, the darn, the darn it comes toe sune!*'

We published his *Ballad of the Goodly Fere,* which must have been his first appearance in a periodical except for contributions to the *Butte Montana Herald.* Ezra, though born there in a caravan during the great blizzard of—but perhaps I ought not to reveal the year. At any rate Ezra left Butte at the age of say two. The only one of his poems written and published there that I can remember had for refrain:

'*Cheer up, Dad!*'

100

As a reaction against a sentiment so American he shortly afterwards became instructor in Romance languages at the University of Pennsylvania. His history up to the date of his appearance in my office which was also my drawing-room comes back to me as follows: Born in the blizzard his first meal consisted of kerosene. That was why he ate such enormous quantities of my tarts, the flavour of kerosene being very enduring. It accounted also for the glory of his hair. Where he studied the Romance languages I could not gather. But his proficiency in them was considerable when you allowed for the slightly negroid accent that he adopted when he spoke Provençal or recited the works of Bertran de Born.

His grandfather I understood was an unsuccessful candidate for the Presidency in the time of Blaine, his father assayer to the Mint in Philadelphia, a function requiring almost incredible delicacy of touch. His grandfather, as was the habit of millionaires in the America of that day, made and lost fortunes with astonishing rapidity and completeness. He had promised to send Ezra to Europe. Ezra was just making his reservations when his grandfather failed more finally and more completely than usual.

Ezra therefore came over on a cattle boat. Many poets have done that. But I doubt if any other ever made a living by showing American tourists about Spain without previous knowledge of the country or language. It was, too, just after the Hispano-American war when the cattle-boat dropped him in that country.

It was with that aura of romance about him that he appeared to me in my office drawing-room. I guessed that he must be rather hard up, bought his poem at once and paid him more than it was usual to pay for ballads. It was not a large sum but Ezra managed to live on it for a long time—six months, I think—in unknown London. Perhaps my pastry helped.

. . . AND D. H. LAWRENCE

In the year when my eyes first fell on words written by Norman Douglas, G. H. Tomlinson, Wyndham Lewis, Ezra Pound, and others, amongst whom was Stephen Reynolds, who died too young and is much too forgotten —upon a day I received a letter from a young school teacher in Nottingham. I can still see the handwriting as if drawn with sepia rather than written in ink, on grey-blue notepaper. It said that the writer knew a young man who wrote, as she thought, admirably but was too shy to send his work to editors. Would I care to see some of his writing?

In that way I came to read the first words of a new author:

'The small locomotive engine, Number 4, came clanking, stumbling down from Selston with seven full wagons. It appeared round the corner with loud threats of speed, but the colt that it startled from among the gorse which still flickered indistinctly in the raw afternoon, outdistanced it in a canter. A woman walking up the railway line to Underwood, held her basket aside and watched the footplate of the engine advancing.'

I was reading in the twilight in the long eighteenth-century room that was at once the office of the *English Review* and my drawing-room. My eyes were tired; I had been reading all day so I did not go any further with the story. It was called *Odour of Chrysanthemums*. I laid it in the basket for accepted manuscripts. My secretary looked up and said:

'You've got another genius?'

I answered: 'It's a big one this time,' and went upstairs to dress. . . .

Miss E.T. in her little book on the youth of Lawrence —and a very charming and serviceable little book it is— seems to be under the impression that she sent me as a first instalment only poems by Lawrence. Actually she first asked me if I would care to see anything—and then should it be poetry or prose. And I had replied asking her to send both, so that she had sent me three poems about a schoolmaster's life . . . and *Odour of Chrysanthemums*. I only mention this because I found the poems, afterwards, to be nice enough but not immensely striking. If I had read them first I should certainly have printed them—as indeed I did; but I think the impact of Lawrence's personality would have been much less vivid. . . . Let us examine, then, the first paragraph of *Odour of Chrysanthemums*.

The very title makes an impact on the mind. You get at once the knowledge that this is not, whatever else it may turn out, either a frivolous or even a gay, springtime story. Chrysanthemums are not only flowers of the autumn; they are the autumn itself. And the presumption is that the author is observant. The majority of people do not even know that chrysanthemums have an odour. I have had it flatly denied to me that they have, just as, as a boy, I used to be mortified by being told that I was affected when I said that my favourite scent was that of primroses, for most people cannot discern that primroses have a delicate and as if muted scent.

Titles as a rule do not matter much. Very good authors break down when it comes to the effort of choosing a title. But one like *Odour of Chrysanthemums* is at once a challenge and an indication. The author seems to say: Take it or leave it. You know at once that you are not going to read a comic story about someone's butler's omniscience. The man who sent you this has, then, character, the courage of his convictions, a power of observation. All these presumptions flit through the mind. At once you read:

'The small locomotive engine, Number 4, came clanking,

stumbling down from Selston,' and at once you know that this fellow with the power of observation is going to write of whatever he writes about from the inside. The 'Number 4' shows that. He will be the sort of fellow who knows that for the sort of people who work about engines, engines have a sort of individuality. He had to give the engine the personality of a number.... 'With seven full wagons'.... The 'seven' is good. The ordinary careless writer would say 'some small wagons.' This man knows what he wants. He sees the scene of his story exactly. He has an authoritative mind.

It appeared round the corner with loud threats of speed.'.... Good writing; slightly, but not *too* arresting.... 'But the colt that it startled from among the gorse... outdistanced it at a canter.' Good again. This fellow does not 'state.' He doesn't say: 'It was coming slowly,' or— what would have been a little better—'at seven miles an hour.' Because even 'seven miles an hour' means nothing definite for the untrained mind. It might mean something for a trainer of pedestrian racers. The imaginative writer writes for all humanity; he does not limit his desired readers to specialists.... But anyone knows that an engine that makes a great deal of noise and yet cannot overtake a colt at a canter must be a ludicrously ineffective machine. We know then that this fellow knows his job.

'The gorse still flickered indistinctly in the raw after-noon....' Good too, distinctly good. This is the just-sufficient observation of Nature that gives you, in a single phrase, landscape, time of day, weather, season. It is a raw afternoon in autumn in a rather accented countryside. The engine would not come round a bend if there were not some obstacle to a straight course—a watercourse, a chain of hills. Hills, probably, because gorse grows on dry, broken-up waste country. They won't also be moun-tains or anything spectacular or the writer would have mentioned them. It is, then, just 'country.'

Your mind does all this for you without any ratiocina-tion on your part. You are not, I mean, purposedly sleuthing. The engine and the trucks are there, with the white smoke blowing away over hummocks of gorse. Yet there has been practically none of the tiresome thing called descriptive nature, of which the English writer is as a rule so lugubriously lavish. . . . And then the woman comes in, carrying her basket. That indicates her status in life. She does not belong to the comfortable classes. Nor, since the engine is small, with trucks on a dud line, will the story be one of the Kipling-engineering type, with gleaming rails, and gadgets, and the smell of oil warmed by the bearings, and all the other tiresomenesses.

You are, then, for as long as the story lasts, to be in one of those untidy, unfinished landscapes where locomotives wander innocuously amongst women with baskets. That is to say, you are going to learn how what we used to call 'the other half'—though we might as well have said other ninety-nine hundredths—lives. And if you are an editor and that is what you are after, you know that you have got what you want and you can pitch the story straight away into your wicker tray with the few accepted manuscripts and go on to some other occupation. . . . Because this man knows. He knows how to open a story with a sentence of the right cadence for holding the attention. He knows how to construct a paragraph. He knows the life he is writing about in a landscape just sufficiently constructed with a casual word here and there. You can trust him for the rest. . . .

I cannot say that I liked Lawrence much. He remained too disturbing even when I got to know him well. He had so much need of moral support to take the place of his mother's influence that he kept one—everyone who at all came into contact with him—in a constant state of solicitude. He claimed moral support imperiously—and physical care too. I don't mean that he whined. He just ordered you to consider that there he was in Croydon subject to the drag of the minds of the school-children for hours of every day in a fetid atmosphere. . . . And that is the great curse and plague of the schoolmaster's life . . . the

105

continuous drag of the minds of the pupils pulling you down ... and then with the tired mind to write master-pieces in the odd moments of silence.

And then came the scourge! He was pronounced tuber-cular. I don't know how we knew that he had been so pronounced. I don't think he ever mentioned it to me; perhaps he did not to anyone. It was a subject that he was always shy of mentioning. But Galsworthy and Masterman and even the solid, stolid Marwood—and of course several ladies—went about for some time with worried faces because Lawrence was writing masterpieces and teaching in a fetid atmosphere. He had to be got out of it. He ought to be allowed to resign his job and be given a pension so that he could go on writing his master-pieces. That was where Masterman, who was a Minister of the Crown and supposed to be scheduled as the next Liberal Prime Minister, came in. He was to use his in-fluence on the educational authorities to see that Law-rence got a pension as having contracted tuberculosis in the service.

Alas, alas, Croydon was not within the Administrative County of London. The London County Council gave pensions to invalided school teachers. But the Surrey County Council did not. Not even the Crown could coerce a county into doing what it did not want to do. ... In the end, I think he was allotted a small lump sum. But one had had a good deal of anxiety.

There had been no difficulty in finding a publisher for him. The odd, accidental, as if *avant la lettre* notoriety that he had gained ... made several publishers be anxious to compete for his suffrages. They even paid him good little sums for his first books. He didn't have then, if ever, any very serious difficulties. And the London of those days was a kind place to people who were reputed to be writing masterpieces. There were kind, very rich people who asked nothing better than to be nice to young men of gifts. So that in a very short time Lawrence was writing home exultantly that he had dined with two Royal

Academicians, several *Times* reviewers, Cabinet Ministers, and Ladies of Title, galore, galore. I don't mean that the exultation was snobbish delight at mingling with the Great. No, it was delight at seeing himself by so far on the road ... towards the two thousand a year....

In the course of a good many Saturday afternoon or Sunday walks in the Gardens or Park, there came home to me a new side of Lawrence that was not father-mother derived—that was pure D.H. It was his passionate—as it were an almost super-sex-passionate—delight in the opening of flowers and leaves. He would see in the blackish grass of Kensington Gardens a disreputable, bedraggled specimen of a poor relation of the dandelion whose name I have forgotten.... Oh, yes, the coltsfoot—the most undistinguished of yellow ornaments of waste places and coal dumps.... And immediately Lawrence, who had been an earnest *jeune homme pauvre* with a foxcoloured poll, drawing wisdom from a distinguished, rather portly editor, would become a half-mad, woodland creature, darting on that poor thing come there by accident, kneeling before it, feeling with his delicate, too white and beautiful fingers, the poor texture of its petals. And describing how, the harbinger of spring, it covered with its sheets of gold the slag-heaps and dumps of his native countryside.... With a really burning language!

And it was not the starved rapture of the Cockney poets to whom flowers were mysteries. He knew the name and the habits and the growths of every flower of the countrysides and of stoats and weasels and foxes and thrushes. Because of course Nottingham, for all its mining suburbs, was really in and of the country, and a great part of the time—the parts of his time when he had really lived—had been spent on the farms that surrounded his home. ... That, of course, you can gather from his books....

Above all from his books. The nature passages of the ordinary English novelist are intolerable—the Dartmoors and Exmoors and Woodlands and the bearded tits and comfreys and the rest. (I am not talking of naturalists.)

But the nature passages of Lawrence run like fire through his books and are exciting—because of the life that comes into his writing even at moments when he is becoming rather tiresomely introspective. So that at times when you read him you have the sense that there really was to him a side that was supernatural . . . in tune with deep woodlands, which are queer places. I rather dislike writing just that because it sounds like the fashionable writing about Lawrence which gloomingly identifies him with Pan—or Priapus or Pisces or phalluses—which you don't find in Nottinghamshire woodlands.

Well. . . . He brought me his manuscripts—those of *The White Peacock* and *Sons and Lovers*. And he demanded, imperiously, immensely long sittings over them . . . insupportably long ones. And when I suggested breathing spaces for walks in the Park he would say that that wasn't what he had sacrificed his Croydon Saturday or Sunday for. And he held my nose down over this passage or that passage and ordered me to say *why* I suggested this emendation or that. And sometimes he would accept them and sometimes he wouldn't . . . but always with a good deal of natural sense and without *parti pris*. I mean that he did not stick obstinately to a form of words because it was his form of words, but he required to be convinced before he would make any alteration. He had learned a great deal from reading other writers—mostly French—but he had a natural sense of form that was very refreshing to come across—and that was perhaps his most singular characteristic. His father was obviously not a dancing teacher and minor craftsman for nothing.

And then one day he brought me half the MS. of *The Trespassers*—and that was the end. It was a *Trespassers* much—oh, but much!—more phallic than is the book as it stands and much more moral in the inverted-puritanic sense. That last was inevitable in that day, and Lawrence had come under the subterranean fashionable influences that made for Free Love as a social and moral arcanum. So that the whole effect was the rather dreary one of a schoolboy larking among placket-holes, dialoguing with a Wesleyan minister who has been converted to Ibsen. It gave the effect that if Lawrence had not met that sort of religion he might have been another ... oh, say, Congreve. As it was it had the making of a thoroughly bad hybrid book and I told him so.

I never saw him again ... to talk to. But he did, in successive re-writings, change the book a good deal ... at least I suppose there were successive re-writings. ... And I suppose I hurt his feelings a good deal. Anyhow I am glad I did not have to go through his manuscripts any more. I don't—and I didn't then—think that my influence was any good to him. His gift for form, in his sort of long book, was such that I could suggest very little to him and the rest of his gift was outside my reach. And, as I have said, he is quite good enough as he is— rich and coloured and startling like a mediaeval manuscript.

THE MARCONI COMMISSION

The only time I wrote about anything political was during the Marconi case. Of that I attended the hearings fairly regularly and I was shocked at the deterioration that appeared to have begun in English public life since the Boer War and the death of Queen Victoria. Before that time a Minister of the Crown was expected to—and usually did—lay down office a poorer man than when he entered public life. That was true too of Germany. Both Bismarck and Gladstone had died poorer than they had been on coming into their inherited wealth. A number of ministers of the first Asquith administration did not however see why a Minister should not use government information when making their investments. They did not indeed see why they should not let their friends in on a good thing. I mean that they really did not see it. Nor did they see any necessity for concealment. Their relatives and intimates called inside financial information one to the other up the very staircases of their clubs.

There was nothing very wonderful in that. After the South African War a wave of financial gambling overcame the country. The great houses in Park Lane fell into the hands of the Randlords as South African speculators who had made good were called. They were received familiarly at Court, became intimates of the highest in the land, won classic races and became national h......

I suppose it was no affair of mine. But perhaps the certainty that the poor old Queen was turning in her grave got on my nerves. At any rate I wrote some impassioned articles backing up Mr F. W. Wilson, the financial editor of the *Outlook*. It was he who really brought about the exposure of the Marconi Affair.

The Postmaster-General was at that date negotiating with the Marconi Company to make a network of Marconi Stations connecting the dominions of the Empire. That much was known to the public and the shares of the Marconi Company rose sympathetically or fell according as the negotiations progressed or stood still. When therefore the relatives and intimates of the Postmaster-General put it about with very little caution among *their* relatives and intimates that the Chancellor of the Exchequer—who ought to be a financial expert—was buying shares in a company subsidiary to the Marconi Company proper the shares of everything connected with wireless telegraphy began extraordinarily to boom and Mr Wilson began his attacks on the Chancellor of the Exchequer, the Postmaster-General and a number of their relatives. The Government at first pooh-poohed the matter. But the agitation spread to other papers and quarters. It became so intense that they had to appoint a Royal Commission to enquire into the whole matter of the sales of Marconi shares.

As I have said, I attended a number of the sittings

of this body. I had before then attended, usually as a witness, a few Royal Commissions. They were non-political and seemed to be conducted with decorum and a fairly efficient if somnolent desire to obtain information. But the Marconi Commission must have been one of the most farcical bodies that ever met. There were seven Liberals and five Tories who voted with the unanimity of the clockwork soldiers of the Russian ballet, each party against the other. The Tories voted that any evidence that could be helpful to the ministers concerned should not be heard, the Liberals that it should. When evidence unfavourable to the ministers was being heard all the Liberals went to sleep in a body; when anything that could be dug up to be favourable to them all the Tories seemed to have been drugged. In addition, Lord Robert Cecil, who presumably suffered from a bad throat, constantly took out an atomiser and opened his mouth extraordinarily wide. The noise of the spray and his vocal garglings would extremely disconcert any ministerial witness.

The evidence was extraordinarily prolix, the repetitions interminable. Gentleman after gentleman swore that he had heard ministerial relatives shouting financial information up the marble staircase of the National Liberal Club; gentleman after gentleman swore that he had not. Financial experts deposed that the shares of companies subsidiary to the parent company would be advantaged by the Postmaster-General's giving a contract to that parent company; financial experts deposed that they would not be in the least advantaged. Everyone in London or New York who had ever heard of anyone else purchasing anything called after Marconi was examined by one side or the other.

At last came the turn of the editor of, I think, the *Financial News*, the journal and its editor having the greatest possible weight in the City. His evidence was not immensely important, mainly because he had been in South America during the greater part of the time when the case had been brewing. When he had finished, the President of the Commission put to him the formal question: Had he anywhere, at any time or in any circumstances heard the name of any other minister who was said to have bought shares in any company connected with Marconi? The editor said that he had not. The chairman, who was bald, white-headed and stout, repeated with extraordinary solemnity, whilst all the Tories snored:

'You have never—at any time, in *any* circumstances, in any place heard mention of any Minister except those whose conduct is here under enquiry as having purchased any shares in any company in any somehow way connected with Marconi's?'

The editor said that he had of course heard idle gossip naming one Minister. But he had means of knowing the names of all purchasers of such stock and knew the gossip was absolutely untrue. All the Liberal members became at once as if galvanised. They insisted on having the name of the accused Minister.

The editor energetically refused to give it. The gossip was perfectly irresistible. He had heard it in a bar in Buenos Aires from a person who in the nature of events could not have private information about the case. And he repeated that he knew the allegation was absolutely untrue.

The Liberals went on pressing him. A Conservative, Mr Amory, made a pointed and impassioned remark about the waste of the Commission's time. The editor refused still. He said he could not as a gentleman be asked to give currency to gossip that he regarded as pestilential lying by the worst type of bar-loafer. His emotion was impressive. The Liberals continued to press him, the Tories to protest. At last the room was cleared for the Commission to put the matter to the vote. The seven Liberals voted for the evidence, the five Tories against its being heard.

The editor was pallid. He protested against being coerced into dishonouring himself. It was no good. He was threatened with the Speaker's writ committing him to the Clock Tower. The whole room hung on his lips in an intense silence. Lord Robert Cecil's spray sounded like artillery; his hanging open jaw gave him the appearance of being about to die. At last the witness said:

'The name was that of Mr Winston Churchill. . . . But I protest. . . .'

That Committee Room at once became like pandemonium. At last the Chairman could be heard to say:

'Mr Churchill must be written to to attend before us,' and we all adjourned to lunch. When we came back there was a long pause, some minutes being inaudibly read. Suddenly there was a roar like that of a charging wild boar. Mr Churchill was pushing aside the people in the doorway as if he had been a forward in a game of football and near the goal. His top hat was pressed down over his ears, his face was as pallid as wax: whiter than the paper on which this is written. His features were so distorted that he was almost unrecognizable. He dashed himself at the chair that was in the horse-shoe shaped space before the Commissioners. He shouted:

'If any man has dared to say that I would do such a damned swinish thing as to buy any share in any filthy company in any way connected with any Governmental action. . . . If any man has dared. . . .'

The chairman said:

'There, there Mr Winston we all know your admirable record.' The Tories hissed in unison: 'An outrage. . . .'

Mr Churchill slammed his fist violently on the table before him and began again:

'If I could get my hands on his throat. . . . To say that I could be capable of such infamy. . . .'

Mr Lloyd George's private secretary dashed up behind him and whispered in his ear. Mr Churchill said:

'I don't care. . . . *Infamy!* . . .' Other ministers' secretaries had a try at him, the humour of the scene being added to by the fact that there was a gangle of acrimonious divorce cases going on among the ministers' secretaries. Mr Asquith was having a great deal of trouble and putting

113

himself to some expense in order to prevent charges and cross-charges making a very pretty scandal and to provide incomes denied to erring partners by recalcitrant and disagreeable parties. I had not considered till then that it was part of the Prime Minister's duties to provide for the lame ducks and divorced wives of his more immediate supporters. But apparently Mr Asquith took the view that it was and behaved with great generosity and kindness. I know this because I was engaged to persuade one of the more unreasonable parties to one of the cases to behave with some moderation.

The final comic relief to the situation was provided by one of the Liberal members who, having begun life by pushing a costermonger's barrow, had lately been ennobled. This knight, who was very handsome in a dark and bearded way, had a singularly sentimental manner and a singular accent. He leaned romantically over the table towards Mr Churchill and made an elaborate oratorical effort. He begged Mr Churchill to be sure that no one in that assembly could so much as most distantly suspect Mr Churchill of financial irregularity. How, he said, could any suspicion of dishonour attach to one descended from the heroic John Churchill, Duke of Marlborough, and one of the greatest generals the world had ever seen?

John Churchill, Duke of Marlborough, had to the common knowledge been one of the greatest eighteenth-century exponents of the art of what is to-day called grafting. So the handsome knight's speech proved too much for the gravity of the meeting and the sitting broke up in some disorder after Mr Churchill with tremendous emphasis had assured the members that, since his taking the smallest office under the Crown, he had not bought a single share in any company whose destinies could be affected by government and before taking such office he had disposed of every such share as happened to be in his possession.

Mr George's speech of exculpation was one of the most marvellous feats of oratorical pathos that could be imagined. Certainly I have never heard on the stage or read in any book anything much more moving. He made no attempt to deny having purchased shares that he ought strictly speaking not to have bought, but he said he had bought them in the usual course of investment and on the advice of his usual financial adviser. He had had nothing to do with any attempts to influence the market. And was, he said, a career of sedulous devotion to the service of his country to be broken because of a mistake that any one not born to opportunities of great experience in the manipulations of shares might easily make?

As he went on he moved the House to deep emotion. A great many of the members—Mr Balfour was one—were moved to tears. I know that I came very near crying myself and in that matter I was as bitter an opponent as Mr George ever had. After the first five minutes of the speech there could be no doubt that the division would be a triumph for him. And it was. He carried practically the whole House with him.

The Marconi Commission had been a grotesque affair and after the sitting which I have described it was summarily brought to an end. But it did undoubtedly have the effect of restoring English public standards to their earlier strictness. I do not believe that any Minister of the Crown has since bought any shares which could in any way be questioned. The horror of having such a body sit interminably on one's case must be enough to deter you from the most minute of irregularities.

A SHAMEFUL EPISODE

I had been then to the Empire to see Miss Génée dance, at a time when seeing Miss Génée dance was one of the great pleasures of my life. There used to be, next door to the old Café Royal, a German beer house called Gambrinius'. There I always went after the theatre, at least when—as I usually was—I was alone. It was vast, decorated with antlers, helmets, *morgensterns*, owls the light of whose eyes went in and out, and the usual decorations that made for a simple Teutonic atmosphere. There was an end, giving on Glasshouse Street, that was rather smart and an end towards Regent Street that was rather Bohemian. When I was in one mood I would go to one end, at other times to the other.

I was sitting then towards the Regent Street end about one in the morning. Towards the other end of the place there was a group of perhaps six or seven waiters and the proprietor, Mr Oddenino, and a member of the public. They were moving chairs, displacing guests, and looking carefully on the floor. I observed near my feet what looked like a large fragment of a beer mug—a dull piece of glass in the sawdust. Then I saw, after I had poked it with my stick, that it was faceted. I picked it up. It seemed duller in my hand than on the ground. It seemed too large to be valuable. I had two regular waiters under whom I sat in that place, the one at one end, the other at the other. The one on the Regent Street side was old, North German, and extremely ugly, the one towards Glasshouse Street was young, Austrian, and cherubic. I asked the old man what the group at the far end were looking for. He said:

'The gentleman has lost a diamond out of his tie-pin.'

I got up and strolled over to that civilian. I say 'civilian' because waiters always impress me as being military overlords of their domains. I held my open hand towards him. I said I supposed that what was in my palm was what he had lost. He jumped at it, as it were, and for a moment was too excited, showing it to the waiters. His tie-pin was noticeable as being, on top of its stick, a large, empty circlet of gold. At last he said to me, quite inoffensively:

'I suppose I could not offer you anything for finding it?'

I said he could not. Then he asked me to sit down and

have a drink with him. I said I would prefer not to. I do not think I ever took a drink with a stranger. Then he said:

'You *must* have a drink with me. Do you know what that stone is? It is the ... diamond.'

It comes back to me as having been the Hope diamond but I daresay it wasn't. It was at any rate one of the famous diamonds of the world of that day. I said that having held the ... diamond in my hand was sufficient reward for having strolled across the café to restore it to him. He said:

'Then come back to Claridge's with me and taste my champagne. I've got some. ...' He named some fabulous brand and vintage year.

When I still refused he said:

'But I'm Harriman.' He added: 'T. E. Harriman.'... I think those were the initials. At any rate they were those of the then railway king of the United States. I said I was as glad to have seen him as to have seen his diamond but that champagne disagreed with me. As a matter of fact I dislike champagne almost more than any other fluid.

I strolled back to my place. But here is the point: I was not half across the café when my little Austrian waiter ran after me and said:

'How could you do it? How *could* you do it? How could you?'

I expressed astonishment. He said, almost crying:

'Why did you give him the diamond? Of course you could not take a reward. But if you had given it to me to give him he must have given me three—four—five hundred pounds, by law. Then I could have opened my café in Wien and married and been happy for ever.'

I was never so ashamed of myself. I have not got over being ashamed of it. Since then I have eaten I suppose the majority of my meals at restaurants—and that lesson I have never forgotten. Waiters, I mean, are human beings and the wise man remembers it.

ALAS!

Two years ago I happened to find in New York my engagement book for 1914. As I had made up my mind to make that city my headquarters from then on I had taken a number of old papers over there in order to sort them out and store them. The engagement book was by chance among them. It was tied up with the soiled, soaked translation into French of my one novel. I had begun to make it in Bécourt-Bécordel wood in July 1916.

The engagement book was an amazing ~~~~~ ~~~~~ From the middle of May to the end of June, except for the week-ends which I spent either at Selsey where I lived next to Masterman and the editor of the *Outlook* or at other people's country houses—there were only six days on which I did not have at least three dinner and after-dinner dates. There would be a dinner, a theatre or a party, a dance. Usually a breakfast at four after that. Or Ezra and his gang carried me off to their night club which was kept by Mme. Strindberg, decorated by Epstein and situate underground.

London was adorable then at four in the morning after a good dance. You walked along the south side of the park in the lovely pearl-grey coolness of the dawn. A sparrow would chirp with a great volume of distinct sound in the silence. Another sparrow, another—a dozen, a hundred, ten thousand. They would be like the violins of an orchestra. Then the blackbirds awakened, then the thrushes, then the chaffinches. It became the sound of an immense choir with the fuller notes of the merle family making obligatos over the chattering counterpoint of the sparrows. Then, as like as not, you turned into the house of some one who had gone before you from the dance to grill sausages and make coffee. Then you breakfasted—usually on the lead roof above a smoking room, giving on to a deep garden. There would be birds there too. Those who cannot remember London then do not know what life holds. Alas. . . .

'MEARY'

THOSE brown, battered men and women of an obscure
Kentish countryside come back to me as the best English
people I ever knew. I do not think that, except for the
parson and the grocer, any one of them could read or
write but I do not believe that one of them ever betrayed
either me or even each other. If, as I undoubtedly do, I
love England with a deep love, though I grow daily more
alien to the Englishman, it is because of them. Here are
some of them:

About twenty-five years ago I wanted some mushroom
catsup. Bonnington was in a scattered, little-populated
village of the south of England. The village stood on what
had formerly been common land; running all down the
side of a range of hills. But this common land had been
long since squatted on, so that it was a maze of little
hawthorn hedges surrounding little closes. Each close had
a few old apple- or cherry-trees, a patch of potato ground,
a cabbage patch, a few rows of scarlet runners, a few
plants of monthly roses, a few plants of marjoram, fennel,
borage, or thyme. And in each little patch there stood a
small dwelling. Mostly these were the original squatters'
huts built of mud, whitewashed outside and crowned with
old thatched roofs on which there grew grasses, house-
leeks, or even irises. There were a great many of these little
houses beneath the September sunshine and it was all a
maze of the small green hedges.

I had been up to the shop in search of my catsup, but
though they sold everything from boots and straw hats to

119

darning needles, bacon, haricot beans, oatmeal, and British wines, they had no catsup. I was wandering desultorily homewards among the small green hedges down hill, looking at the distant sea seven miles away over the marsh. Just beyond a little hedge I saw a woman digging potatoes in the dry, hot ground. She looked up as I passed and said:

'Hullo, Measter!'

I answered: 'Hullo, Missus!' and I was passing on when it occurred to me to ask her whether she knew anyone who sold catsup. She answered:

'Naw! Aw doon't knaw na sarl'

I walked on a little farther and then sat down on a stile for half an hour or so; enjoying the pleasant weather and taking a read in the country paper which I had bought in the shop. Then I saw the large, stalwart old woman coming along the stony path carrying two great trugs of the potatoes that she had dug up. I had to get down from the stile to let her pass. And then seeing that she was going my way, that she was evidently oldish and was probably tired, I took the potato trugs from her and carried them. She strode along in front of me between the hedges. She wore an immense pair of men's hob-nailed boots that dragged along the stones of the causeway with metallic sounds, an immense shawl of wool that had been beaten by the weather until it was of a dull liver colour, an immense skirt that had once been of lilac cotton print, but was now a rusty brown, and an immense straw hat that had been given her by some one as being worn out and that had cost twopence when it was new. Her face was large, as round and much the same colour as a copper warming-pan. Her mouth was immense and quite toothless except for one large fang, and as she smiled cheerfully all the time, her great gums were always to be seen. Her shoulders were immense and moved with the roll and heave of those of a great bullock. This was the wisest and upon the whole the most estimable human being that I ever knew at all well. Her hands were enormous and

stained a deep blackish green over their original copper
colour by the hops that it was her profession to tie.

As we walked along she told me that she was exactly the
same age as our Queen who was then just seventy. She
told me also that she wasn't of those parts but was a
Paddock Wood woman by birth, which meant that she
came from the true hop country. She told me also that her
husband had died fifteen years before of the sting of a
viper, that his poor old leg went all like green jelly up to
his thigh before he died, and that he had been the best
basket-maker in all Kent. She also told me that we can't
all have everything and that the only thing to do is to
'keep all on gooing.'

I delivered up her trugs to her at her garden gate and
she said to me with a cheerful nod:

'Well I'll do the same for you mate, when you come to
be my age.' She shambled over the rough stone of her
garden path and into her dark door beneath the low thatch
that was two yards thick. Her cottage was more dilapidated
than any that I have ever seen in my life. It stood in a very
long narrow triangle of ground, so that the hedge that I
walked along must have been at least eighty yards in length,
while at its broadest part the potato patch could not have
measured twenty spade breadths. But before I was come
to the end of the hedge her voice was calling out after me:

'Measter! Dun yo really want ketchup?'

I replied that I really did.

She said:

'Old Meary Spratt up by Hungry Hall wheer ye see me
diggin'—she makes ketchup.'

I asked her why she had not told me before and she
answered,

'Well, ye see the Quality do be asking foolish questions,
I thought ye didn't really want to know.'

I learnt afterwards it wasn't only the dislike of being
asked foolish questions. In Meary Walker's long, wise life
she had experienced one thing—that no man with a collar
and a tie is to be trusted. She had had it vaguely in her

mind that, when I asked the question, I might be some sort of excise officer trying to find out where illicit distilling was carried on. She didn't know that the making of catsup was not illegal. She had heard that many of her poor neighbours had been fined heavily for selling bottles of home-made sloe-gin or mead. She had refused to answer, out of a sense of automatic caution for fear she should get poor old Meary Spratt into trouble.

But next morning she turned up at my cottage carrying two bottles of Meary Spratt's catsup in an old basket covered with a cloth. And after that, seeing her rather often at the shop on Saturday nights when all the world came to buy its Sunday provisions, and because she came in to heat the bake-oven with faggots once a week, and to do the washing—in that isolated neighbourhood, among the deep woods of the Weald, I got to know her as well as I ever knew anybody. This is her biography:

She was the daughter of a day labourer among the hop-fields of Paddock Wood. When she had been born, the youngest of five, her own mother had died. Her father had brought a stepmother into the house. I never discovered that the stepmother was notably cruel to Meary. But those were the Hungry 'Forties. The children never had enough to eat. Once, Meary cut off one of her big toes. She had jumped down into a ditch after a piece of turnip peel. She had of course had no shoes or stockings and there had been a broken bottle in the ditch.

So her childhood had been a matter of thirst, hunger, and frequent chastisements with the end of a leather strap that her father wore round his waist. When she was four-teen she was sent to service in a great house where all the maids slept together under the roof. Here they told each other legends at night—odd legends that exactly resembled the fairy tales of Grimm—legends of princes and princesses, of castles, or of travelling companions on the road. A great many of these stories seemed to hinge upon the price of salt which at one time was extravagantly dear in the popular memory, so that one princess offered to have her heart cut out in order to purchase a pound of salt that should restore her father to health.

From this house Meary Walker ran away with a gipsy— or at least he was what in that part of the world was called a 'pikey'—a user of the turnpike road. So, for many years they led a wandering existence, until at last they settled down in this village. Until the date of that settlement Meary had not troubled to marry her Walker. Then a parson insisted on it, but it did not trouble her much either way.

Walker had always been a man of weak health. He had what is called the artistic temperament—a small, dark, delicate man whose one enthusiasm was his art of making baskets. In that he certainly excelled. But he was lazy and all the work of their support fell on Meary. She tied hops— and this is rather skilled work,—she picked them in the autumn; she helped the neighbours with baking and brewing. She cleaned up the church once a week. She planted the potatoes and cropped them. She was the first cottager in East Kent to keep poultry for profit. In her biography you could find traces of great benevolence and of considerable heroism. Thus, one hard winter, she supported not only herself and her husband, but her old friend Meary Spratt, at that time a widow with six children. Meary Spratt was in bed with pneumonia and its after effects, from December to March. Meary Walker nursed her, washed and tended the children, and made the livings for all of them.

Then there came the time when she broke her leg and had to be taken against her will to the hospital which was seven miles away. She did not want to be in the hospital; she was anxious to be with Walker who was then dying of gangrene of the leg. She was anxious too about a sitting hen; one of her neighbours had promised her half a crown for a clutch of chickens. She used to lie in hospital, patting her broken knee under the bedclothes and exclaiming:

'Get well, get well, oh do get well quickly!' And even twenty years afterwards when she rehearsed these scenes and these words there would remain in the repetition a whole world of passionate wistfulness. But indeed, she translated her passion into words. One night, driven beyond endurance by the want of news of Walker and of her sitting hen she escaped from the hospital window and crawled on her hands and knees the whole seven miles from the hospital to her home. She found when she arrived in the dawn that Walker was in his coffin. The chickens however were a healthy brood. Her admiration for Walker, the weak and lazy artist in basket-making, never decreased. She treasured his best baskets to the end of her life, as you and I might treasure Rembrandts. Once, ten years after, she sat for a whole day on his grave. The old sexton, growing confused with years, had made a mistake and was going to inter another man's wife on top of Walker. Meary stopped that.

For the last twenty-six years or so of her life she lived in the mud hut which I had first seen her enter. She went on as before, tying hops, heating ovens, picking up stones, keeping a hen or two. She looked after, fed and nursed—for the love of God—a particularly disagreeable old man called Purdey who had been a London cab-driver. He sat all day in a grandfather's chair, grumbling and swearing at Meary whenever she came in. He was eighty-two. He had no claim whatever upon her and he never paid her a penny of money.

So she kept on going all through life. She was always cheerful: she had always on her tongue some fragment of peasant wisdom. Once, coming back from market, she sat down outside a public-house and a soldier treated her to a pot of beer. Presently there rode up the Duke of Cambridge in his field-marshal's uniform and beside him there was the Shah of Persia. They were watching a sham fight in the neighbourhood. Meary raised her pot of beer towards these royal personages and wished them health. They nodded in return.

'Well,' Meary called out to the Duke, 'you're only your mother's son like the rest of us.'

Once, Batalha Reis amiably told her that, in his language, bread was 'pom.' She expressed surprise, but then she added:

'Oh, well poor dear, when you're hungry you've got to eat it, like the rest of us, whatever you call it.'

She was sorry for him because he had to call bread by such an outlandish name. She could not think how he remembered the word. Yet she knew that *Brot* was the German for bread and *Apfel* for apples, because, during the Napoleonic Wars, the Hanoverian Legion had garrisoned that part of the country and there remained until the accession of Queen Victoria. One of what she called the jarman legions had murdered his sweetheart, who had been a friend of her mother's, and when he was hung for it at Canterbury he asked for *Brot* and *Apfel* on the scaffold. She saw him hung, a pleasant fair boy, and when she looked down at her hands she said they were white as lard.

So she worked on until she was seventy-eight. One day she discovered a swelling under her left breast. It gave her no pain but she wanted to know what it was. So she put a hot brick to it. She knew that if it was cancer that was a bad thing to do, but she wanted to get it settled. The swelling became worse. So she walked to the hospital—the same hospital that she had crawled away from. They operated on her next morning—and she was dead by noon. Her last words were:

'Who's going to look after old Purdey?'

CAREW AND OTHER TRAMPS

It puzzled me for many years to know what castles in Spain a tramp built—what was *his* particular Island of the Blest; and after getting over the first shyness of accosting these slightly repellent bundles of clothes (for it is, after all, the clothes that repel us), I pursued this ideal with some diligence. It was Carew, the tramp, who got me most easily over my shyness. He was a man of no particular book-learning, though he said that hardly a day passed without his picking up a paper. He was the son of a Guardsman and a prostitute, and his professional tale had it that he had been bred up as a tooth-comb maker; machines had destroyed *that* occupation. He carried a comb in his pocket; but I fancy that he delighted to comb his long golden beard, and had the comb for that purpose, inventing the profession to fit the implement. I have met him in Regent's Park, on the Sussex Downs, in Cornwall, and in the Strand; but he always carried his boots under his arm—I never knew quite why. I fancy it was on account of some superstition: he did not like boots, but a sort of luck, I imagine, clung to this particular pair. An odd mixture of sardonic candour and savage reticence, he would admit to having been in every gaol in the south of England, but he would never reveal what he was afraid of on the roads at night. He always crept into the shelter of some house at nightfall, and he had once, he told me, been arrested for following a young lady five miles across Salisbury Plain in the moonlight—with no other evil purpose than the desire to keep a human being in sight.

In spite of the comb, he said he had never done a day's work in his life, and never meant to. He lay by the roadside, and sometimes he had been so magnificently lazy that he had gone without food for two days rather than beg. 'You get sick of people's faces at times,' he said.

But Carew, as far as I can discover, built no castles in Spain. He supposed that pneumonia would carry him off one of these days, probably in China, as he styled Lewes gaol. He called the various prisons by the names of countries, and nick-named workhouses after the great cities of the world. Thus Eachend Hill Union was Paris with him, and Bodmin, Rome; though this caused confusion, because, of course, London itself is Rome in the lingo of the hedgerows. His crimes, as far as I know, were limited to sleeping out; in this flagrant offence he was very frequently taken because of the nervous tendency which made him sleep in stack-yards near cattle, or in farm stables near horses, for the sake of company. He exhibited with a pride a small sheaf of newspaper cuttings which recorded his convictions, and his insolent retorts to magistrates. He was delighted with these; but he seemed to have no further ambitions. He was as contented with a 'bob' as with a 'quid' if I gave it him, and apparently contented with a 'brown.' He let life roll by in front of him, and took from it as little as he gave.

If you stay for any time at an inn looking down on one of the great tramp highways, you will see the same faces, the same clothes, the same battered hats, the same splay feet, pass and repass your window at intervals of a day or two; for many of these tramps, having found a string of two or three comfortable wards, will spend, like summer ghosts, the whole of the warm season haunting the same countryside. Congenital lack of candour, the desire to please their interlocutor, sheer muzziness of brain, or sheer ferocity, make it difficult to discover what may be the ideal of this brown flotsam. Their universal and official shibboleth has it that if they could only get a steady job and a nice little cottage they would settle down with the missus and kids and live respectable under the parson for evermore. The more candid of the men, when they were assured that their reply would make no difference in the number of coppers destined for them, confessed almost without exception that their ideal was to have a pension like a soldier. This appeared to be, as it were, the good establishment that every middle-class man wishes for his daughter. As a matter of fact, a very considerable percentage of the innumerable old soldiers who solicit alms along the road do have such pensions, and for perhaps three glorious nights out of the month are kings of the earth—kings over draggled and carneying subjects, as aware as their monarch himself of when pay-day comes round, and where the floodgates of oblivion will be let loose.

One very hot day last month, on a high-road broad and parched, stretching out level and without end beneath an empty sky, on a day so hot that the very larks were silent, and the twittering duologue of the linnets sounded as if it came from dusty little throats, I sat down in the long grass under the hedge by the side of a very inviting and swarthy tramp. He suddenly brought out in a rich soft voice, without any inquiry of mine—

'Lord! I'd like to be a workhouse master, I'd like to be the master of a workhouse! Wouldn't I give the casuals champagne and porterhouse steaks one day, and wouldn't I wollup them the next!'

A little time before I had walked along the same road in a drenching rain with a German tramp, tiny, wizened, ferret-faced, and with the extravagant gestures of an actor. With his right hand he held firmly to my sleeve, and from a great scroll of manuscript in his left he read passages from a poem about the beauties of nature abounding in the forest near the town of Carlsruhe in Baden. His whole being was engrossed in his work, he saw neither road, sky, nor sea; only from time to time he broke off to exclaim, 'This is very pleasant, you will like this very much!' His life-history, varied and unromantic as it was, would occupy too much space in the telling, but *his* consoling thought was that Wagner had been too poor to possess an overcoat whilst he was writing his music drama of *Rienzi*; and hope, ardour, confidence, and romance were in his eyes and voice when, at saying farewell to me, he uttered the words: 'There is a Russian author, I forget his name, who has just bought an estate on the Volga for 700,000 marks; once he was only a tramp like me.' He was quite illiterate and his poem was atrocious, but he said that people on the road were very kind to him; one gentleman at Brighton had given him board and lodging for three nights.

Thus between the fragrant hedgerows the townsman newly come into his heart of the country will see this vast body of dun-coloured units driven backwards and forwards like ghosts upon the tides of the winds. For him, indeed, they must remain ghosts; as a rule he will feel the repulsion that we must all feel for those who are outside our world, outside our life, outside our praise, outside our banning or our cursing.

They are as much outside pity or regret as are the innumerable dead; they have gone back into the heart of the country and have become one with the ravens, the crows, the weasels, and the robins, picking up the things that we have no use for, from such small parcels of grounds as we have not enclosed.

To the really inveterate townsman every weather-beaten man or woman that he passes along the road is a tramp. It is as difficult for him to distinguish a genuine waggoner from a fraudulent tooth-comb maker as to tell rye grass from permanent pasture, or the mistle from the song-thrush. But gradually as he sinks deeper into the life of the country, passes during weeks and months between hedgerows and begins to note differences between the songs of birds, he will acquire a sort of instinctive knack of distinguishing between one sort and the other. The differences lie in minute things, in the poise of the head, the way of setting down the foot, the glance of the eye in passing. The townsman may make experiments in reclaiming the tramp—like Hercules he will wrestle with death for possession of one soul—but once the man is really dead there is no recalling him. He may set him up and endow him with tools, clothes, a place to live in, and all the fair simulacra of our corporate life; he may keep him propped up for a day, for a week, for a month, for a year, but sooner or later the body will collapse and the soul once more be at one with the Maker of the hedgerow. To try preventing the real tramp from following out his life is like attempting to stifle the words of a poet or the sighs of a miserable lover. But if he ever come to examine meticulously, the townsman will discover that amongst these ghosts there whirl past some that still cling to life, that claim our pity and need such helping hands as the gods will let us give. Once, when I lived on a hillside below a common, I came home in the evening down through the furze and saw a faded old man and a faded old woman, with the usual perambulator of the traveller, encamped in a small sandpit. They were both painfully clean, and beneath an arbour of gorse bushes had an odd air of being Philemon and Baucis cast upon an unsympathetic world, where the very twilight of the gods had passed away. But what struck me most and most disagreeably was to see my own favourite yellow Orpington cock dancing up and down in front of the old man full a quarter of a mile away from my gate. I imagined that he was one of those people who can whisper poultry out of a field, just as gipsies are said to do with stallions. But on reaching home I saw my cock contentedly dusting himself in an ash-heap, and when I went a couple of hours later to the post, passing the old people's settlement, I saw that the yellow cock had been reinforced by a gigantic lop-eared rabbit, an aged tortoise-shell cat, and a battered accordion. These were the Lares and Penates of this ancient couple, the signs that, evil days having fallen upon them and the hatred of the workhouse having forced them to take the road, they still clung desperately to as much as they could carry in a perambulator of their former householder's dignity; they still clung desperately to life, the old man still hoping for fruit-trees to prune, the old woman still cherishing her ideal of many beehives to look after.

TABLE TALK

MYSELF

In a mild way I should call myself a sentimental Tory and a Roman Catholic.

GOOD FRIDAY

Good Friday before last I gave a lunch to four men at my London club. I passed the meat as a matter of habit, of good manners, of what you will. What was my astonishment to discover that each of my guests passed the meat. In short each of us five was actually a Roman Catholic of a greater or less degree of earnestness. Yet, although we were all five fairly intimate, meeting frequently and talking of most of the things that men talk about, we were not any one of us aware of the other's religious belief. This, I think, would be impossible anywhere but in London, and it is just for that reason that London of to-day is such a restful place to live in.

ROSSETTI'S INVERNESS CAPE

Upon Rossetti's death, his inverness, which was made in the year 1869, descended to my grandfather. Upon my grandfather's death it descended to me, it being then twenty-three years old. I wore it with feelings of immense pride as if it had been—and indeed was it not?—the mantle of a prophet. And such approbation did it meet with in my young friends of that date that this identical garment was copied seven times, and each time for the use of a gentleman whose works, when Booksellers Row still existed, might ordinarily be found in the Twopenny Box. So this garment spread the true tradition, and indeed it was imperishable and indestructible, though what has become of it by now I do not know. I wore it for several years until it must have been aged probably thirty, when, happening to wear it during a visit to my tailor's, and telling that gentleman in common with history, I was distressed to hear him remark, looking over his pince-nez:

'Time the moths had it!'

This shed such a light upon the garment from the point of view of tailors that I never wore it again. It fell, I am afraid, into the hands of a family with little respect for relics of the great, and I am fairly certain that I observed its capacious folds in the mists of an early morning upon Romney Marsh some months ago, enveloping the limbs of an elderly and poaching scoundrel called Slingsby.

A FABIAN DEBATE

I remember being present at a Fabian debate as to the attributes of the Deity. I forget what it was all about, but it lasted a very considerable time. Towards the end of the meeting an energetic lady arose—it was, I think, her first attendance at a Fabian meeting—and remarked:

'All this talk is very fine, but what I want to know is, whether the Fabian Society does, or does not, believe in God?'

A timid gentleman rose and replied:

'If Mrs Y—— will read Fabian Tract 312, she will discover what she ought to think upon this matter.'

THE MUSIC STOPPED

The other day I was at a wedding reception—there was a very large crowd. In one corner an excellent quintette discussed selections from the *Contes d'Hofmann*. We were all talking twenty to the dozen. My *vis-à-vis* was telling me something that did not interest me, when the voice of a man behind me said: 'So they left him there in prison with a broken bottle of poison in his pocket.' And then the music stopped suddenly and I never heard who the man was, or what he had done to get into prison, or why he had broken the bottle of poison.

STRAWBERRY JAM AND OYSTERS

The other day I attended a concert consisting mainly of the Song Cycles of Debussy, setting the words of Verlaine. They were sung by an Armenian lady who had escaped from a Turkish harem and had had no musical training. She was a barbaric creature who uttered loud howls, and the effect was to me disagreeable in the extreme; all the same, the audience was large and enthusiastic and the most enlightened organ of musical opinion of to-day spoke of the performance with a chastened enthusiasm. I happened to meet the writer of the notice in the course of the following afternoon, and I asked him what he really got for himself out of that singular collocation of sounds. He said airily: 'Well, you see, one gets emotions!'

I said: 'Good God! what sort of emotions?'

He answered: 'Well, you see, if one shuts one's eyes one can imagine that one is eating strawberry jam and oysters in a house of ill-fame, and a cat is rushing violently up and down the keyboard of the piano with a cracker tied to its tail.'

I said: 'Then why in the world didn't you say so in your notice?'

He smiled blandly:

'Well, you see, an ignorant public might take such a description for abuse, and we cannot afford to abuse anything now.'

PRE-RAPHAELITE LOVE

Love, according to the Pre-Raphaelite canon, was a great but rather sloppy passion. Its manifestations would be Paolo and Francesca, or Launcelot and Guinevere. It was a thing that you swooned about on broad, general lines, your eyes closed, your arms outstretched. It excused all sins, it sanctified all purposes and, if you went to hell over it, you still drifted about amongst snow-flakes of fire with your eyes closed and in the arms of the object of your passion. For it is impossible to suppose that when Rossetti painted his picture of Paolo and Francesca in hell, he, or any of his admirers, thought that these two lovers were really suffering. They were not. They were suffering perhaps with the malaise of love which is always an uneasiness, but an uneasiness how sweet! And the flakes of flames were descending all over the rest of the picture, but they did not fall upon Paolo and Francesca. No, the lovers were protected by a generalized, swooning passion that formed, as it were, a moral and very efficient macintosh all over them. And no doubt what D. G. Rossetti and his school thought was that, although guilty lovers have to go to hell for the sake of the story, they will find hell pleasant enough because the aroma of their passion, the wings of the great god of love and the swooning intensity of it all will render them insensible to the inconveniences of their lodgings. As much as to say that you do not mind the bad cooking of the Brighton hotel if you are having otherwise a good time of it.

ON OBSOLETE WORDS

I remember once hearing Stephen Crane—the author of *The Red Badge of Courage* and of *The Open Boat*, which is the finest volume of true short stories in the English language—I remember hearing him, with his wonderful eyes flashing and his extreme vigour and intonation, comment upon a sentence of Robert Louis Stevenson that he was reading. The sentence was: 'With interjected finger he delayed the motion of the timepiece.' 'By God, poor dear!' Crane exclaimed. 'That man put back the clock of English fiction fifty years.' I do not know that this is exactly what Stevenson did do. I should say myself that the art of writing in English received the numbing blow of a sandbag when Rossetti wrote, at the age of eighteen, *The Blessed Damozel*. From that time forward and until to-day—and for how many years to come!—the idea has been inherent in the mind of the English writer that writing was a matter of digging for obsolete words with which to express ideas for ever dead and gone. Stevenson did this, of course, as carefully as any Pre-Raphaelite, though instead of going to mediaeval books he ransacked the seventeenth century. But this tendency is unfortunately not limited to authors misusing our very excellent tongue. The other day I was listening to an excellent Italian *conférencier* who assured an impressed audience that Signor D'Annunzio is the greatest Italian stylist there has ever been, since in his last book he has used over 2,017 obsolete words which cannot be understood by a modern Italian without the help of a mediaeval glossary.

MR RUSKIN'S EPITHET

On one page of one of Mr Ruskin's books I have counted the epithet 'golden' six times. There are 'golden days,' 'golden-mouthed,' 'distant golden spire,' 'golden peaks' and 'golden sunset,' all of them describing one picture by Turner in which the nearest approach to gold discernible by a precise eye is a mixture of orange red and madder brown.

MIXING UP NAMES

Nothing can prevent my mixing up names. I suppose I inherit the characteristic from my grandfather, who had it to a dangerous degree. I would come in and say to him:

'Grandpa, I met Lord Leighton in the Park and he sent his regards to you.' He would exclaim with violence: 'Leighton! How dare you be seen talking to him? And how dare he presume to send messages to me? He is the scoundrel who...' I would interrupt:

'But, Grandpa, he is the President of the Royal Academy....' He would interrupt in turn: 'Nonsense. I tell you he is the fellow who got seven years for....' A few minutes after he would exclaim:

'Leighton? Oh, Leighton? Why didn't you say Leighton if you meant Leighton. I thought you said Fothergill-Bovey Haines. Of course there is no reason why you should not be civil to Leighton.'

WALTER CRANE'S GLOVES

I moved back to the Pent which I had let to an artist then of some fame. His name being Crane he had painted a bird of that species on the front door which gave on to the stockyard beyond a narrow strip of terrace and lawn. He had also painted numbers on all the room-doors. There were thirteen. His family used to take baths on the lawn which worried and astonished the stockmen and shepherds in the yards below. When they left there remained behind them an extraordinary number of gloves. In every drawer of the bedrooms there were old, soiled and crumpled gloves. I have remained wondering to this day what they can have been wanting with so many. Is there a *maladie de gants* as there is said to be of boots? At any rate we used them all to manure the roots of a vine that covered the front of the house. Leather is the best of all manures for vines and also for figs. Indeed if you want to plant a fig tree you should plant it with its roots in an old leather portmanteau. You will have wonderful figs.

THE CITY OF DREADFUL NIGHT

Those were grim enough times for artists—the 'eighties and early 'nineties. I don't know that they are any better now. There was a blind poet called Philip Bourke Marston. He was not a very striking poet, but because he was blind he occupied a position of some note amongst the minor Pre-Raphaelite group. He was bearded like an elder statesman of those days and, with his down-glancing eyes, was of noble appearance. Members of the group used to take it in turns to read to him in his gloomy room in the Euston Road. One day another poet of much greater reputation came in. He threw a fit of delirium tremens and imagined himself a Bengal tiger; he fell upon poor Marston and mauled him rather severely, the blind man being unable to defend himself at all. William Sharpe came in and found them struggling on the floor. He pulled off the dipsomaniac who immediately burst a blood vessel, his blood pouring all over both Marston and Fiona Macleod. Sharpe ran around to the nearby hospital to fetch a doctor. The physician in charge immediately cried out that Sharpe must be arrested for murder. He was drunk. In the meantime, the dipsomaniac bled to death and Marston nearly went out of his mind. . . . Yes, grim times in that city of dreadful night!

MAUPASSANT AND THE NAKED LADY

Mr James recounted that once, when Mr James had been invited to lunch with him, Maupassant had received him, not, be assured, in a dressing-gown, but in the society of a naked lady wearing a mask.... And Maupassant assured the author of *The Great Good Place* that the lady was a *femme du monde*. And Mr James believed him.... Fortune could go no further than *that*!...

A NOVELIST'S CREDO

The first thing the novelist has to learn is self-effacement —that first and that always. Not for him flowing locks, sombreros, flaming ties, eccentric pants. If he gets himself up like a poet humanity will act towards him as if he were a poet... disagreeably. That would not matter were it not that he will see humanity under a false aspect. Then his books will be wrong.

His effort should be to be at one with his material. Without that he will not understand the emotions and reactions of his human renderings. Superstitions, belief in luck, premonitions, play such a great part in human motives that a novelist who does not to some extent enter into those feelings can hardly understand and will certainly be unable to render to perfection most human affairs. Yes, you must sacrifice yourself. You must deny yourself the pleasure of saying to your weaker brothers and sisters: 'Haw! No superstitions about me.' Indeed you must deny yourself the pleasure of high-hatting anybody about anything. You must live merrily and trust to good letters.

POEMS

ON HEAVEN

To V.H., who asked for a working Heaven

I

That day the sunlight lay on the farms;
On the morrow the bitter frost that there was!
That night my young love lay in my arms,
   The morrow how bitter it was!

And because she is very tall and quaint
And golden, like a *quattrocento* saint,
I desire to write about Heaven;
To tell you the shape and the ways of it,
And the joys and the toil in the maze of it,
For these there must be in Heaven,
Even in Heaven!

For God is a good man, God is a kind man,
And God's a good brother, and God is no blind man,
And God is our father.

     I will tell you how this thing began:
How I waited in a little town near Lyons many years,
And yet knew nothing of passing time, or of her tears,
But, for nine slow years, lounged away at my table in the
    shadowy sunlit square
Where the small cafés are.

The *Place* is small and shaded by great planes,
Over a rather human monument
Set up to *Louis Dixhuit* in the year
Eighteen fourteen; a funny thing with dolphins
About a pyramid of green-dripped, sordid stone.
But the enormous, monumental planes
Shade it all in, and in the flecks of sun

Sit market women. There's a paper shop
Painted all blue, a shipping agency,
Three or four cafés; dank, dark colonnades
Of an eighteen-forty *Maîrie*. I'd no wish
To wait for her where it was picturesque,
Or ancient or historic, or to love
Over well any place in the land before she came
And loved it too. I didn't even go
To Lyons for the opera; Arles for the bulls,
Or Avignon for glimpses of the Rhône.
Not even to Beaucaire! I sat about
And played long games of dominoes with the *maître*,
Or passing *commis-voyageurs*. And so
I sat and watched the trams come in, and read
The *Libre Parole* and sipped the thin, fresh wine
They call Piquette, and got to know the people,
The kindly, southern people . . .

Until, when the years were over, she came in her swift
    red car,
Shooting out past a tram; and she slowed and stopped and
    lighted absently down,
A little dazed, in the heart of the town;
And nodded imperceptibly.
With a sideways look at me.

So our days here began.

And the wrinkled old woman who keeps the café,
And the man
Who sells the *Libre Parole*,
And the sleepy gendarme,
And the fat *facteur* who delivers letters only in the shady,
Pleasanter kind of streets;
And the boy I often gave a penny,
And the *maître* himself, and the little girl who loves toffee
And me because I have given her many sweets;
And the one-eyed, droll

Bookseller of the *rue Grand de Provence*,—
Chancing to be going home to bed,
Smiled with their kindly, fresh benevolence,
Because they knew I had waited for a lady
Who should come in a swift, red, English car,
To the square where the little cafés are.
And the old, old woman touched me on the wrist
With a wrinkled finger,
And said: 'Why do you linger?—
Too many kisses can never be kissed!
And comfort her—nobody here will think harm—
Take her instantly to your arm!
It is a little strange, you know, to your dear,
To be dead'!

But one is English,
Though one be never so much of a ghost;
And if most of your life has been spent in the craze to
      relinquish
What you want most,
You will go on relinquishing,
You will go on vanquishing
Human longings, even
In Heaven.

God! You will have forgotten what the rest of the world
      is on fire for—
The madness of desire for the long and quiet embrace,
The coming nearer of a tear-wet face;
Forgotten the desire to slake
The thirst, and the long, slow ache,
And to interlace
Lash with lash, lip with lip, limb with limb, and the fingers
      of the hand with the hand
And . . .

You will have forgotten . . .

                              But they will all awake;

Aye, all of them shall awaken
In this dear place.
And all that then we took
Of all that we might have taken,
Was that one embracing look,
Coursing over features, over limbs, between eyes, a making
    sure, and a long sigh,
Having the tranquillity
Of trees unshaken,
And the softness of sweet tears,
And the clearness of a clear brook
To wash away past years.
(For that too is the quality of Heaven,
That you are conscious always of great pain
Only when it is over
And shall not come again.
Thank God, thank God, it shall not come again,
Though your eyes be never so wet with the tears
Of many years!)

II

And so she stood a moment by the door
Of the long, red car. Royally she stepped down,
Settling on one long foot and leaning back
Amongst her russet furs. And she looked round . . .
Of course it must be strange to come from England
Straight into Heaven. You must take it in,
Slowly, for a long instant, with some fear . . .
Now that *affiche*, in orange, on the kiosque:
'*Six Spanish bulls will fight on Sunday next
At Arles, in the arena*' . . . Well, it's strange
Till you get used to our ways. And, on the *Mairie*,
The untidy poster telling of the *concours
De vers de soie*, of silkworms. The cocoons
Pile, yellow, all across the little Places
Of ninety townships in the environs

Of Lyons, the city famous for her silks.
What if she's pale? It must be more than strange,
After these years, to come out here from England
To a strange place, to the stretched-out arms of me,
A man never fully known, only divined,
Loved, guessed at, pledged to, in your Sussex mud,
Amongst the frost-bound farms by the yeasty sea.
Oh, the long look; the long, long searching look!
And how my heart beat!
                              Well, you see, in England
She had a husband. And four families—
His, hers, mine, and another woman's too—
Would have gone crazy. And, with all the rest,
Eight parents, and the children, seven aunts
And sixteen uncles and a grandmother.
There were, besides, our names, a few real friends,
And the decencies of life. A monstrous heap!
They made a monstrous heap. I've lain awake
Whole aching nights to tot the figures up!
Heap after heaps, of complications, griefs,
Worries, tongue-clackings, nonsenses and shame
For not making good. You see the coil there was!
And the poor strained fibres of our tortured brains,
And the voice that called from depth in her to depth
In me . . . my God, in the dreadful nights,
Through the roar of the great black winds, through the
      sound of the sea!
Oh agony! Agony! From out my breast
It called whilst the dark house slept, and stairheads creaked;
From within my breast it screamed and made no sound;
And wailed . . . And made no sound.
And howled like the damned . . . No sound! No sound!
Only the roar of the wind, the sound of the sea,
The tick of the clock . . .
And our two voices, noiseless through the dark.
O God! O God!

(That night my young love lay in my arms . . .

There was a bitter frost lay on the farms
In England, by the shiver
And the crawling of the tide;
By the broken silver of the English Channel,
Beneath the aged moon that watched alone—
Poor, dreary, lonely old moon to have to watch alone,
Over the dreary beaches mantled with ancient foam
Like shrunken flannel;
The moon, an intent, pale face, looking down
Over the English Channel.

But soft and warm One lay in the crook of my arm,
And came to no harm since we had come quietly home
Even to Heaven;
Which is situate in a little old town
Not very far from the side of the Rhône,
That mighty river
That is, just there by the Crau, in the lower reaches,
Far wider than the Channel.)

But, in the market place of the other little town,
Where the Rhône is a narrower, greener affair,
When she had looked at me, she beckoned with her long,
       white hand,
A little languidly, since it is a strain, if a blessed strain, to
       have just died.
And, going back again,
Into the long, red, English racing car,
Made room for me amongst the furs at her side.
And we moved away from the kind looks of the kindly
       people
Into the wine of the hurrying air.
And very soon even the tall grey steeple
Of Lyons cathedral behind us grew little and far
And then was no more there . . .
And, thank God, we had nothing any more to think of,
And, thank God, we had nothing any more to talk of;
Unless, as it chanced, the flashing silver stalk of the pampas
Growing down to the brink of the Rhône,

On the lawn of a little chateau, giving onto the river.
And we were alone, alone, alone...
At last alone...

The poplars on the hill-crests go marching rank on rank,
And far away to the left, like a pyramid, marches the ghost
    of Mont Blanc.
There are vines and vines and vines, all down to the
    river bank.
There will be a castle here,
And an abbey there;
And huge quarries and a long, white farm,
With long thatched barns and a long wine shed,

As we ran alone, all down the Rhône.
And that day there was no puncturing of the tyres to fear;
And no trouble at all with the engine and gear;
Smoothly and softly we ran between the great poplar alley
All down the valley of the Rhône.
For the dear, good God knew how we needed rest and to
    be alone.
But, on other days, just as you must have perfect shadows
    to make perfect Rembrandts,
He shall afflict us with little lets and hindrances of His own
Devising—just to let us be glad that we are dead...
Just for remembrance.

III

Hard by the castle of God in the Alpilles,
In the eternal stone of the Alpilles,
There's this little old town, walled round by the old, grey
    gardens...
There were never such olives as grow in the gardens of
    God,
The green-grey trees, the wardens of agony
And failure of gods.
Of hatred and faith, of truth, of treachery

They whisper; they whisper that none of the living prevail;
They whirl in the great mistral over the white, dry sods,
Like hair blown back from white foreheads in the enormous
    gale
Up to the castle walls of God . . .

But, in the town that's our home,
Once you are past the wall,
Amongst the trunks of the planes,
Though they roar never so mightily overhead in the day,
All this tumult is quieted down, and all
The windows stand open because of the heat of the night
That shall come.
And, from each little window, shines in the twilight a light,
And, beneath the eternal planes
With the huge, gnarled trunks that were aged and grey
At the creation of Time,
The Chinese lanthorns, hung out at the doors of hotels,
Shimmering in the dusk, here on an orange tree, there on
    a sweet-scented lime,
There on a golden inscription: 'Hotel of the Three Holy
    Bells.'
Or 'Hotel Sublime,' or 'Inn of the Real Good Will.'
And, yes, it is very warm and still,
And all the world is afoot after the heat of the day,
In the cool of the even in Heaven . . .
And it is here that I have brought my dear to pay her all
    that I owed her,
Amidst this crowd, with the soft voices, the soft footfalls,
    the rejoicing laughter.
And after the twilight there falls such a warm, soft darkness,
And there will come stealing under the planes a drowsy
    odour,
Compounded all of cyclamen, of oranges, or rosemary and
    bay,
To take the remembrance of the toil of the day away.

So we sat at a little table, under an immense plane,
And we remembered again

The blisters and foments
And terrible harassments of the tired brain,
The cold and the frost and the pain,
As if we were looking at a picture and saying: 'This is true!
Why this is a truly painted
Rendering of that street where—you remember?—I
    fainted.'
And we remembered again
Tranquilly, our poor few tranquil moments,
The falling of the sunlight through the panes,
The flutter for ever in the chimney of the quiet flame,
The mutter of our two poor tortured voices, always
    a-whisper
And the endless nights when I would cry out, running
    through all the gamut of misery, even to a lisp, her
    name;
And we remembered our kisses, nine, maybe, or eleven—
If you count two that I gave and she did not give again.

And always the crowd drifted by in the cool of the even,
And we saw the faces of friends,
And the faces of those to whom one day we must make
    amends,
Smiling in welcome.
And I said: 'On another day—
And such a day may well come soon—
We will play dominoes with Dick and Evelyn and Frances
For a whole afternoon.
And, in the time to come, Genée
Shall dance for us, fluttering over the ground as the sun-
    light dances.'
And *Arlésiennes* with the beautiful faces went by us,
And gipsies and Spanish shepherds, noiseless in sandals of
    straw, sauntered nigh us,
Wearing slouch hats and old sheep-skins, and casting
    admiring glances
From dark, foreign eyes at my dear . . .
(And ah, it is Heaven alone, to have her alone and so near!)

149

So all this world rejoices
In the cool of the even
In Heaven ...
And, when the cool of the even was fully there,
Came a great ha-ha of voices.
Many children run together, and all laugh and rejoice and
    call,
Hurrying with little arms flying, and little feet flying, and
    little hurrying haunches,
From the door of a stable,
Where, in an *olla podrida*, they had been playing at the
    corrida
With the black Spanish bull, whose nature
Is patience with children. And so, through the gaps of the
    branches
Of jasmine on our screen beneath the planes,
We saw, coming down from the road that leads to the
    olives and Alpilles,
A man of great stature,
In a great cloak,
With a great stride,
And a little joke
For all and sundry, coming down with a hound at his side.
And he stood at the cross-roads, passing the time of day
In a great, kind voice, the voice of a man-and-a-half!—
With a great laugh, and a great clap on the back,
For a fellow in black—a priest I should say,
Or may be a lover,
Wearing black for his mistress's mood.
'A little toothache,' we could hear him say; 'but that's so
    good
When it gives over.' So he passed from sight
In the soft twilight, into the soft night,
In the soft riot and tumult of the crowd.

And a magpie flew down, laughing, holding up his beak
    to us.

150

And I said: 'That was God! Presently, when he has walked
    through the town
And the night has settled down,
So that you may not be afraid,
In the darkness, he will come to our table and speak to us.'
And past us many saints went walking in a company—
The kindly, thoughtful saints, devising and laughing and
    talking,
And smiling at us with their pleasant solicitude.
And because the thick of the crowd followed to the one
    side God,
Or to the other the saints, we sat in solitude.
In the distance the saints went singing all in chorus,
And our Lord went by on the other side of the street,
Holding a little boy.
Taking him to pick the musk-roses that open at dusk,
For wreathing the statue of Jove,
Left on the Alpilles above
By the Romans; since Jove,
Even Jove,
Must not want for his quota of honour and love;
But round about him there must be,
With all its tender jollity,
The laughter of children in Heaven,
Making merry with roses in Heaven.

Yet never he looked at us, knowing that that would be
    such joy
As must be over-great for hearts that needed quiet;
Such a riot and tumult of joy as quiet hearts are not able
To taste to the full . . .

. . . And my dear one sat in the shadows; very softly she
    wept:—
Such joy is in Heaven,
In the cool of the even,
After the burden and toil of the days,
After the heat and haze

In the vine-hills; or in the shady
Whispering groves in high passes up in the Alpilles,
Guarding the castle of God.

And I went on talking towards her unseen face:
'So it is, so it goes, in this beloved place,
There shall be never a grief but passes; no, not any;
There shall be such bright light and no blindness;
There shall be so little awe and so much loving-kindness;
There shall be a little longing and enough care,
There shall be a little labour and enough of toil
To bring back the lost flavour of our human coil;
Not enough to taint it;
And all that we desire shall prove as fair as we can paint it.'
For, though that may be the very hardest trick of all
God set Himself, who fashioned this goodly hall.
Thus He has made Heaven;
Even Heaven.

For God is a very clever mechanician;
And if He made this proud and goodly ship of the world,
From the maintop to the hull,
Do you think He could not finish it to the full,
With a flag and all,
And make it sail, tall and brave,
On the waters, beyond the grave?
It should cost but very little rhetoric
To explain for you that last, fine, conjuring trick;
Nor does God need to be a very great magician
To give to each man after his heart,
Who knows very well what each man has in his heart:
To let you pass your life in a night-club where they dance,
If that is your idea of heaven; if you will, in the South of
    France;
If you will, on the turbulent sea; if you will, in the peace
    of the night;
Where you will; how you will;
Or in the long death of a kiss, that may never pall:

He would be a very little God if He could not do all this,
And He is still
The great God of all.

For God is a good man; God is a kind man;
In the darkness He came walking to our table beneath the
        planes,
And spoke
So kindly to my dear,
With a little joke,
Giving Himself some pains
To take away her fear
Of His stature,
So as not to abash her,
In no way at all to dash her new pleasure beneath the planes,
In the cool of the even
In Heaven.

That, that is God's nature.
For God's a good brother, and God is no blind man,
And God's a good mother and loves sons who're rovers,
And God is our father and loves all good lovers.
He has a kindly smile for many a poor sinner;
He takes note to make it up to poor wayfarers on sodden
        roads;
Such as bear heavy loads
He takes note of, and of all that toil on bitter seas and
        frosty lands,
He takes care that they shall have good at His hands;
Well He takes note of a poor old cook,
Cooking your dinner;
And much He loves sweet joys in such as ever took
Sweet joy on earth. He has a kindly smile for a kiss
Given in a shady nook.
And in the golden book
Where the accounts of His estate are kept,
All the round, golden sovereigns of bliss,
Known by poor lovers, married or never yet married,

Whilst the green world waked, or the black world quietly
    slept;
All joy, all sweetness, each sweet sigh that's sighed—
Their accounts are kept,
And carried
By the love of God to His own credit's side.
So that is why He came to our table to welcome my dear,
    dear bride,
In the cool of the even
In front of a café in Heaven.

1914

ANTWERP

I

Gloom!
An October like November;
August a hundred thousand hours,
And all September,
A hundred thousand, dragging sunlit days,
And half October like a thousand years . . .
And doom!
That then was Antwerp . . .
                    In the name of God,
How could they do it?
Those souls that usually dived
Into the dirty caverns of mines;
Who usually hived
In whitened hovels; under ragged poplars;
Who dragged muddy shovels, over the grassy mud,
Lumbering to work over the greasy sods . . .
Those men there, with the appearances of clods
Were the bravest men that a usually listless priest of God
Ever shrived . . .
And it is not for us to make them an anthem.
If we found words there would come no wind that would
    fan them
To a tune that the trumpets might blow it,
Shrill through the heaven that's ours or yet Allah's
Or the wide halls of any Valhallas.
We can make no such anthem. So that all that is ours
For inditing in sonnets, pantoums, elegiacs, or lays
Is this:
In the name of God, how could they do it?'

II

For there is no new thing under the sun,
Only this uncomely man with a smoking gun

In the gloom . . .
What the devil will he gain by it?
Digging a hole in the mud and standing all day in the rain
    by it
Waiting his doom,
The sharp blow, the swift outpouring of the blood,
Till the trench of grey mud
Is turned to a brown purple drain by it.
Well, there have been scars
Won in many wars . . .
Punic,
Lacedaemonian, wars of Napoleon, wars for faith, wars for
    honour, for love, for possession,
But this Belgian man in his ugly tunic,
His ugly round cap, shooting on, in a sort of obsession,
Overspreading his miserable land,
Standing with his wet gun in his hand . . .
Doom!
He finds that in a sudden scrimmage,
And lies, an unsightly lump on the sodden grass . . .
An image that shall take long to pass!

III

For the white-limbed heroes of Hellas ride by upon their
    horses
For ever through our brains.
The heroes of Cressy ride by upon their stallions;
And battalions and battalions and battalions—
The Old Guard, the Young Guard, the men of Minden
    and of Waterloo,
Pass, for ever staunch,
Stand for ever true;
And the small man with the large paunch,
And the grey coat, and the large hat, and the hands behind
    the back,

Watches them pass
In our minds for ever . . .
But that clutter of sodden corses
On the sodden Belgian grass—
That is a strange new beauty.

IV

With no especial legends of marchings or triumphs or duty,
Assuredly that is the way of it,
The way of beauty . . .
And that is the highest word you can find to say of it.
For you cannot praise it with words
Compounded of lyres and swords,
But the thought of the gloom and the rain
And the ugly coated figure, standing beside a drain,
Shall eat itself into your brain.
And that shall be an honourable word;
'Belgian' shall be an honourable word,
As honourable as the fame of the sword,
As honourable as the mention of the many-chorded lyre,
And his old coat shall seem as beautiful as the fabrics
     woven in Tyre.

V

And what in the world did they bear it for?
I don't know.
And what in the world did they dare it for?
Perhaps that is not for the likes of me to understand.
They could very well have watched a hundred legions go
Over their fields and between their cities
Down into more southerly regions.
They could very well have let the legions pass through
    their woods,

And have kept their lives and their wives and their
    children and cattle and goods.
I don't understand.
Was it just love of their land?
Oh poor dears!
Can any man so love his land?
Give them a thousand thousand pities
And rivers and rivers of tears
To wash off the blood from the cities of Flanders.

VI

This is Charing Cross;
It is midnight;
There is a great crowd
And no light.
A great crowd, all black that hardly whispers aloud.
Surely, that is a dead woman—a dead mother!
She has a dead face;
She is dressed all in black;
She wanders to the bookstall and back,
At the back of the crowd;
And back again and again back,
She sways and wanders.

This is Charing Cross;
It is one o'clock.
There is still a great cloud, and very little light;
Immense shafts of shadows over the black crowd
That hardly whispers aloud . . .
And now! . . . That is another dead mother,
And there is another and another and another . . .
And little children, all in black,
All with dead faces, waiting in all the waiting-places,
Wandering from the doors of the waiting-room
In the dim gloom.

These are the women of Flanders.
They await the lost.
They await the lost that shall never leave the dock;
They await the lost that shall never again come by the
    train
To the embraces of all these women with dead faces;
They await the lost who lie dead in trench and barrier and
    foss,
In the dark of the night.
This is Charing Cross; it is past one of the clock;
There is very little light.

There is so much pain.

L'Envoi.
And it was for this that they endured this gloom;
This October like November,
That August like a hundred thousand hours,
And that September,
A hundred thousand dragging sunlit days,
And half October like a thousand years . . .
Oh poor dears!

1915

VIEWS

I

Being in Rome I wonder will you go
Up to the Hill. But I forget the name . . .
Aventine? Pincio? No: I do not know.
I was there yesterday and watched. You came.

The seven Pillars of the Forum stand
High, stained and pale 'neath the Italian heavens,
Their capitals linked up form half a square;
A grove of silver poplars spears the sky.
You came. Do you remember? Yes, you came,
But yesterday. Your dress just brushed the herbs
That nearly hide the broken marble lion . . .
And I was watching you against the sky.
Such light! Such air! Such prism hues! and Rome
So far below; I hardly knew the place.
The domed St Peter's; mass of the Capitol;
The arch of Trajan and St Angelo . . .
Tiny and grey and level; tremulous
Beneath a haze amidst a sea of plains . . .
But I forget the name, who never looked
On any Rome but this of unnamed hills.

II

Tho' you're in Rome you will not go, my You,
    Up to that Hill . . . But I forget the name,
Aventine? Pincio? No, I never knew . . .
    I was there yesterday. You never came.

I have that Rome; and you, you have a Me,
You have a Rome and I, I have my You;
My Rome is not your Rome: my you, not you
                    . . . For, if man knew woman

I should have plumbed your heart; if woman, man
Your me should be true I . . . If in your day—
You who have mingled with my soul in dreams,
You who have given my life an aim and purpose,
A heart, an imaged form—if in your dreams
You have imagined unfamiliar cities
And me among them, I shall never stand
Beneath your pillars or your poplar groves . . .
Images, simulacra, towns of dreams
That never march upon each other's borders
And bring no comfort to each other's hearts!

III

Nobly accompanied am I—Since you,
You—simulacrum, image, dream of dreams,
Amidst these images and simulacra
Of shadowy house fronts and these dim, thronged streets
Are my companion!
              Where the pavements gleam
I have you alway with me: and grey dawns
In the far skies bring you more near—more near
Than City sounds can interpenetrate.
All vapours form a background for your face
In this unreal town of real things,
And my you stands beside me and makes glad
All my imagined cities and thence walks
Beside me towards yet unimagined hills . . .
Being we two, full surely we shall go
Up to that Hill . . . some synonym for Home.
Avalon? Grave? or Heaven? I do not know . . .
But one day or today, the day may come,
When I may be your I, your Rome my Rome.

1910

'WHEN THE WORLD WAS IN BUILDING ...'

Thank Goodness, the moving is over,
They've swept up the straw in the passage
And life will begin ...
This tiny, white, tiled cottage by the bridge! ...
When we've had tea I will punt you
To Paradise for the sugar and onions
We will drift home in the twilight,
The trout will be rising ...

1918